# GERMANY

## A PRIMARY SOURCE CULTURAL GUIDE

**Ann Byers**

The Rosen Publishing Group's
**PowerPlus Books™**
New York

*To Doug and Vanessa, whose love began in Germany*

Published in 2005 by The Rosen Publishing Group, Inc.
29 East 21st Street, New York, NY 10010

First Edition

**Library of Congress Cataloging-in-Publication Data**

Byers, Ann.
Germany/Ann Byers.—1st ed.
    p. cm.—(Primary sources of world cultures)
Includes bibliographical references and index.
Contents: The land—The people—The German language—German myths and legends—German festivals and ceremonies of antiquity and today—The religions of Germany throughout its history—The art and architecture of Germany—The literature and music of Germany—Famous foods and recipes of Germany—Daily life and customs in Germany—Education and work in Germany.
ISBN 1-4042-2910-8 (library binding)
1. Germany--Juvenile literature. [1. Germany.] I. Title. II. Series.

DD17.B94 2005
943—dc22

                                                                                    2003027570

*Manufactured in the United States of America*

**Cover images:** Background: A letter written and signed by the German writer and poet Johann Christoph Friedrich von Schiller. Left: The German Reichstag in Berlin, Germany. Right: Bavarian children wearing traditional dress.

**Photo credits:** cover (background), pp. 52, 83 (top) © Hulton/Archive/Getty Images; cover (middle), p. 115 © Jan-Peter Boening/Laif/Aurora Photos; cover (bottom) © Dallas and John Heaton/Corbis; pp. 3, 118, 120 © GeoAtlas; pp. 4 (top), 8, 10, 15, 48 (top) © Topham/The Image Works; pp. 4 (middle), 36 © Julia Knop/Laif/Aurora Photos; pp. 4 (bottom), 56 (top) © Masakatsu Yamazaki/HAGA/The Image Works; pp. 5 (top), 85 © Fogel François/Corbis Sygma; pp. 5 (middle), 39, 42, 99 © Kruell/Laif/Aurora Photos; pp. 5 (bottom), 74, 109, 113 © Laif/Aurora Photos; p. 6 © Doug Scott/Age Fotostock; p. 7 © Frank Chmura/Image State; p. 9 © Gaby Gerster/Laif/Aurora Photos; pp. 11, 93 (top) © Thomas Hoepker/Magnum Photos; p. 12 © Willy Matheisl/Age Fotostock; pp. 13, 24 (bottom), 93 (bottom), 103 © Sven Martson/The Image Works; pp. 14, 16 (bottom) © Konrad Wothe/Minden Pictures; p. 16 (top) © Engel & Gielen/plus 49/The Image Works; p. 17 (top) © Norbert Rosing/National Geographic Image Collection; p. 17 (bottom), 87 © AFP/Getty Images; p. 18 © Steve Vidler/SuperStock; p. 19 © Victoria & Albert Museum, London/Art Resource, NY; pp. 20, 29, 46, 47, 54, 55, 78, 80, 84 (bottom) © Mary Evans Picture Library; p. 21 (bottom) © The Stapleton Collection/Bridgeman Art Library; p. 22 © Chateau de Versailles, France/Bridgeman Art Library; pp. 23, 69, 72, 76, 82 (bottom) © Erich Lessing/Art Resource, NY; pp. 24 (top), 44 © North Wind Picture Archives; p. 25 © Historical Picture Archive/Corbis; p. 26 © Archives Charmet/Bridgeman Art Library; p. 27 © Scala/Art Resource, NY; p. 28 © Key Color/Index Stock Imagery; pp. 30 (top), 61 (bottom), 79 (top) © Private Collection/Bridgeman Art Library; p. 30 (bottom) © The Art Archive/National Archives, Washington D.C.; p. 31 © Yevgeny Khaldei/Corbis; p. 32 (top) © Burt Glinn/Magnum Photos; p. 32 (bottom) © Raymond Depardon/Magnum Photos; p. 33 © Rene Burri/Magnum Photos; pp. 35, 58, 65 (top), 66, 70, 110 © Peter Essick/Aurora Photos; pp. 37, 100 © Marco Pesaresi/Contrasto/Redux; p. 38 © Biskup/Laif/Aurora Photos; p. 40 © The Art Archive/University Library Heidelberg/Dagli Orti; p. 41 (top) © James L. Amos/National Geographic Image Collection; p. 41 (bottom) © Ken Welsh/Bridgeman Art Library; p. 45 © Akira Nakata/HAGA/The Image Works; p. 48 (bottom) © Treasury of Monza Cathedral, Italy/Bridgeman Art Library; p. 49 (top) © Edwin Wallace/Mary Evans Picture Library; pp. 50, 89 © Hideo Haga/HAGA/The Image Works; pp. 51, 57 © Shinichi Wakatsuki/HAGA/The Image Works; p. 53 © Bill Bachmann/The Image Works; p. 56 (bottom) © Adam Tanner/The Image Works; pp. 60, 71 (bottom), 77, 107, 108 © SuperStock; p. 61 (top) © Art Resource, NY; p. 62 © Hilbich/akg-images; p. 64 © Hughes/Laif/Aurora Photos; p. 65 (bottom) © Sasse/Laif/Aurora Photos; p. 67 © Bridgeman Art Library, London/SuperStock; p. 68 © Bayerische Staatsbibliothek, Munich, Germany/Bridgeman Art Library; p. 71 (top) © The Art Archive/Musco del Prado, Madrid; p. 75 © The Art Archive/São Paulo Art Museum, Brazil/Dagli Orti; p. 81 (top) © Alinari/Art Resource, NY; p. 81 (bottom) © National Portrait Gallery, London/SuperStock; p. 82 (top) © 2003 Charles Walker/Topfoto/The Image Works; p. 83 (bottom) © Photofest; p. 84 (top) © The Art Archive/Karl Marx Museum Trier/Dagli Orti (A); p. 86 © Marion Kalter/akg-images; p. 88 © Hausch-StockFood Munich/StockFood; p. 90 © Josef Polleross/The Image Works; p. 91 (top) © Guenter Beer/VISUM/The Image Works; p. 91 (bottom) © Wendy Sue Lamm/Contrasto/Redux; p. 92 © Köb, Ulrike/StockFood; p. 94 © Holger Stamme/Okapia/Photo Researchers; p. 95 © Lee Snider/The Image Works; pp. 96, 106 © Stuart Cohen/The Image Works; p. 97 © Walter Geiersperger/Photri/Microstock; p. 98 © Horacek/Bilderberg/Aurora Photos; p. 99 (bottom) © Margot Granitsas/The Image Works; p. 101 (top) © The Kobal Collection; p. 101 (bottom) © Sony Pictures Classics/The Kobal Collection/Spauke, Bernd; pp. 102, 114 © Paul Langrock/Laif/Aurora Photos; p. 104 © Mette/Laif/Aurora Photos; p. 105 © Dirk Eisermann/Laif/Aurora Photos; p. 111 © Steinhilber/Bilderberg/Aurora Photos; p. 112 © Bettmann/Corbis; p. 119 © Matton.

# CONTENTS

# INTRODUCTION

F ew nations of the world have been so characterized by constant change as Germany has. Its borders, its government, and its people have shifted and evolved countless times over the centuries. Dramatic social, economic, and political shifts continue to define Germany in the twenty-first century.

The area the ancient Romans called Germania was originally bounded by the Rhine and Danube Rivers on the west and south but had no clear limits to the east. However, the borders on all sides of the country moved or disappeared altogether as a result of migrations, wars, and alliances among various tribes. At various times in its history, Germany filled all or parts of the nine nations that now surround it—Denmark, the Netherlands, Belgium, Luxembourg, France, Switzerland, Austria, the Czech Republic, and Poland.

Part of Germany's fascination lies in its rich cultural history. Many of the Western world's most cherished pieces of classical music sprang from Germany, the birthplace of Ludwig van Beethoven, Johann Sebastian Bach, and Johannes Brahms. Germany also produced great writers and philosophers whose ideas shaped the world. Since the Middle Ages, when German monks copied and taught the ancient texts, Germany has been recognized as an important center of learning and the arts.

At left, Neuschwanstein Castle, built between 1869 and 1886, was designed by King Ludwig II of Bavaria to resemble a medieval fairy-tale castle. The castle was dedicated to Ludwig's favorite operatic composer, Richard Wagner, and was largely inspired by Wagner's works. Above, a member of a traditional Bavarian oompah band stands with his two sons. They are dressed in traditional Bavarian clothes, including lederhosen.

The medieval town of Rothenburg is Germany's best preserved walled town. In medieval times, it was Germany's second-largest city. Rothenburg is situated along the Romantic Road that runs through Bavaria, connecting Frankfurt and Munich. The Romantic Road is famous for its medieval towns, castles, and breathtaking views of the Alps.

Yet there is also a very dark side to German history and culture. While Germany has made enormous contributions to civilization, it is also the country of the barbarian tribes that brought down the Roman Empire. It is the nation that began and lost two devastating and bloody world wars in the twentieth century. It is the land that produced and sustained Adolf Hitler, the Nazi Party, and the concentration camps in which 6 million Jews and 5 to 6 million other persecuted minorities were killed during World War II (1939–1945). This darkest period of German history is known as the Holocaust.

During and after the Second World War, the last great shifting of Germany's borders, government, and citizens took place. From 1939 to 1990, Germany's boundaries changed at least four times. First, German soldiers pushed their borders far into neighboring countries at the outset of World War II. In the waning days of the war, Allied soldiers (composed mainly of American, British, French, and Soviet forces) took back the land Germany had occupied and pared the country down to the smallest it had ever been. These four nations occupied Germany's capital city,

Frankfurt has been the financial center of Germany for hundreds of years. The city is home to the Frankfurt Stock Exchange, European Central Bank, and Bundesbank (Germany's central bank). Because of its financial reputation, the city has acquired the nickname "Bankfurt."

Berlin, until peace and order could be restored. In 1949, the Soviet Union forced the division of Germany into two separate nations—the Federal Republic of Germany (democratic West Germany) and the German Democratic Republic (Communist East Germany).

Finally, in 1990, East and West Germans came together and reunified the country. Since then, Germany has remained stable. It has clearly defined borders and a democratic constitution. As an important member of the European Union, it contributes to the economy and security of the entire continent. Today, Germany is a strong and responsible nation at the heart of Europe.

# THE LAND

## The Geography, Climate, and Wildlife of Germany

I f two lines were drawn diagonally across the European continent—one from Iceland in the northwest to the island of Crete in the southeast, the other from the northeastern extreme of the Ural Mountains in Russia to the south-western edge of Spain—the lines would intersect in Germany. Germany is at the very center of Europe.

It is not a very big country. Covering 137,744 square miles (almost 357,000 square kilometers), Germany is only the size of Montana. But it is bigger than all nine nations that surround it except for France. To the north, the Baltic Sea and the North Sea form a natural boundary. Between the two bodies of water, Germany shares a short, 42-mile (68 km) border with Denmark. Poland and the Czech Republic are to the east, and Switzerland and Austria are to the south. Germany's longest border is on the west. Along this 828-mile (1,333 km) stretch lie the Netherlands, Belgium, Luxembourg, and France.

Germany is composed of sixteen states, or *Länder* (the singular is *Land*). They are: Baden-Württemberg, Bavaria, Berlin, Brandenburg, Bremen, Hamburg, Hessen, Mecklenburg–Vorpommern, Lower Saxony, North Rhine–Westphalia, Rhineland-Palatinate, Saarland, Saxony, Saxony-Anhalt, Schleswig-Holstein, and Thuringia.

At left, Saint Colomon Church is situated in the scenic foothills of the Bavarian Alps, home to hundreds of picturesque churches and castles. Above, the hills of Saxony are technically not mountains, but they are sometimes referred to as the Saxon Alps. Saxony borders Poland, the Czech Republic, and the German states of Bavaria, Thuringia, Saxony-Anhalt, and Brandenburg.

One of Germany's finest gothic cathedrals, St. Peter's rises above the Danube River in Regensburg. The Danube River is the second-longest river in Europe (the Volga is the longest) and flows through ten countries, including Austria, Bulgaria, Croatia, Germany, Hungary, Moldova, Slovakia, Romania, Ukraine, and Serbia and Montenegro.

## Rivers

Germany is crossed by several rivers. Most begin in the mountains and flow north into the North Sea or Baltic Sea. The exception is the Danube, which is the only major river on the continent to flow from west to east. It is the main water transportation route from western Europe to eastern Europe. It takes the manufactured goods of Germany as far as the Black Sea and brings the agricultural wealth of the Balkan countries (such as Serbia, Croatia, Albania, and Bosnia) into Germany. The Rhine, Weser, Elbe, and Oder Rivers are important north–south transportation routes. All the large rivers are linked together by a network of canals.

Probably the most important waterway of all Europe is the one the Germans call Father Rhine. It begins as a small stream high in the Alps. Fed by melting snow and glaciers, it winds westward from Lake Constance and plummets 75 feet (23 meters) over a breathtaking waterfall. Then it turns north, carving deep gorges and fertile valleys before twisting west through the Netherlands to the North Sea. Its southernmost portion is called the Upper Rhine because it is in the mountains; the Rhine's northern stretch is known as the Lower Rhine.

The Rhine River flows through Worms in Rhineland-Palatinate. The name "Worms" derives from a Celtic word that means "settlement in a watery area." "Rhine" is also derived from a Celtic word, meaning "to flow."

The 35-mile (56 km) section between the towns of Bingen and Koblenz is known as the Middle Rhine. The well-watered valley of the Middle Rhine produces grapes that are used to make the region's world-famous wines. The cliffs along this portion of the river are lined with more castles than any other area in the world. The Rhine courses through all of Germany's five geographic regions: the Alps, the Alpine Foreland, the Southwest Uplands, the Central Uplands, and the Northern Lowlands.

## Geographic Regions

The Alps, perhaps the best known of Germany's landscapes, occupies only a thin sliver of the southern edge of the country. The Bavarian Alps contain Germany's highest point, the Zugspitze (9,718 feet, or 2,962 meters). The Alps make up the upper (mountainous) region of the Land of Bavaria, or Bayern, from the southern city of Munich. Its picture-postcard meadows, pastures, and tiny villages are dwarfed by majestic, snow-clad peaks.

Lower Bavaria and part of the Land of Baden-Württemberg are in the Alpine Foreland, a high trough between mountain ranges. The foreland consists of the Swabian-Bavarian highlands and the Danube River basin. This is an area of rounded hills, large lakes, and broad plains. It contains several marshy moors. The waters of these marshes have been used for centuries as therapeutic baths. The area is primarily rural, its poor soil used for pastureland rather than farming.

The Southwest Uplands region is divided from the Alpine Foreland by two mountain chains between the Danube and Main Rivers: the Swabian and Franconian Albs. From the Black Forest at the extreme southwest of Germany, these ranges curve north 250 miles (400 km) almost to the border with the Czech Republic in the east. They are much lower than the Alps, nowhere higher than about 3,280 feet (1,000 m). The streams and rivers on one side of the Alps flow into the Danube, and the waters on the other side empty into the Rhine.

The Southwest Uplands occupy parts of three Länder: Baden-Württemberg, Bavaria, and Rhineland-Palatinate, or Rheinland-Pfalz. The Upper Rhine and its tributary, the Neckar River, give life to the southwest. The fertile valleys of the two rivers are terraced and green with orchards and vineyards. The Upper Rhine valley is flanked by mountain forests. West of the river is the Palatinate Forest of the Hardt Mountains. On the east are the Oden and Black Forests.

The Black Forest, which spreads over 2,000 square miles (5,180 sq km) of mountains, gets its name from the thick groves of fir trees on the upper slopes. At lower elevations, oak and beech trees grow. Unfortunately, acid rain—precipitation that carries industrial pollutants—has destroyed as many as half the forest's trees. The forest contains many lakes and mineral springs that have been made into health resorts. It is known for its small farms, cattle raising, toy production, and cuckoo clocks.

North of the Swabian and Franconian Albs, a wide belt of highlands called the Central Uplands divides northern Germany from southern Germany. It is part of a band of low mountain ranges that stretches across Europe from France to Poland and the Czech Republic. The Central Uplands encompass the German Länder of Saarland, Hessen, and Thuringia as well as part of Rhineland-Palatinate; much of North Rhine–Westphalia, Saxony, Lower Saxony, and Saxony-Anhalt; and a portion of eastern Bavaria. The mountains of the Central Uplands are covered with forests at lower elevations. Above the tree lines are many barren, marshy moors.

Along Germany's western edge, two rivers—the Rhine and the Moselle—carve beautiful, deep

The Black Forest, inspiration for so much of Germany's folklore, is also a popular recreation area for campers, hikers, and skiers.

A woman harvests grapes in a vineyard in the village of Bacharach. The wines of Bacharach are considered some of the best in the Rhineland-Palatinate region.

valleys through the mountains of the Central Uplands. The middle and north Rhine valleys and the Moselle valley are among the most scenic in all of Europe. Along the lower banks of the rivers, grapevines grow in abundance and quaint villages built in the Middle Ages hold wine festivals. On the upper slopes, castle towers and cathedral spires peek out from dense thickets of pine and fir.

Where the mountains of the Central Uplands drop to flat land, the Northern Lowlands begin. This region takes in the Länder of Schleswig-Holstein, Hamburg, Bremen, Mecklenburg–Vorpommern, Brandenburg, and Berlin as well as parts of Saxony, Lower Saxony, Saxony-Anhalt, and North Rhine–Westphalia. Its terrain is quite varied. Along the foothills of the upland mountain ranges, the rich soil and mild climate make the southern lowland the breadbasket of Germany. Farther north, marshy floodplains alternate with heaths and moors. The terrain of the North Sea is marshy and flat, whereas the western Baltic coast has steep cliffs deeply pitted by fjords (inlets of the sea passing between steep cliffs). Offshore are islands that at one time were part of the mainland.

The great variation of Germany's terrain is illustrated by how the land is used. About one-third of the nation's land is cultivated, another third consists of forests and woodlands, and about 17 percent is meadow and pastureland. The rest is covered by urban and suburban development.

## Climate

Since Germany, like Canada, is located above the forty-seventh parallel in latitude, it might be expected to be very cold. However, winds that are warmed by the Gulf Stream blow across the lowlands from the North Sea. As a result, all of north and northwestern Germany enjoys a maritime climate of warm summers and mild winters. Away

The red and white striped Westerhever Lighthouse is located in Schleswig-Holstein. Situated in ecologically sensitive mudflats, it is one of the North Frisian region's best known landmarks.

from the seashore, most of Germany has a continental climate. This means that the weather is moderate but a little cooler than the maritime areas in the winter and a little warmer in summer. Mountainous areas of the south have greater extremes because the elevation is higher. The mean temperature for the entire country is 48° Fahrenheit (9°C). The ocean winds carry a good deal of moisture, and rain falls—as does snow in the late fall, winter, and early spring—year-round in Germany. Average yearly precipitation is 24 to 32 inches (61 to 81 centimeters), although in the mountains of the south it is about 79 inches (201 cm).

## Wildlife and Natural Resources

At one time, the fields and forests of Germany were filled with wildlife. Centuries of hunting and cutting down trees, however, have reduced the animal population con-

siderably. Today, thirteen national parks and more than 6,300 nature reserves have been created to restore some of the country's natural beauty and preserve remaining and endangered animal and plant species.

Deer and wild boar still roam the forests as they did in ancient times, but laws now restrict the numbers that can be hunted. Alongside these game animals can be found foxes, wild rabbits, squirrels, weasels, and wild cats. Raccoons, although not native to Germany, established themselves there after being brought from North America. The lynx population, once reduced to zero in Germany, has rebounded in the eastern forests. Songbirds and woodpeckers are plentiful in the mountain forests.

The wild boar is a kind of pig with a thick, bristly coat and an aggressive temperament. Because wild boars raid and destroy crops and gardens, they are often hunted by farmers. Boar hunting is an ancient tradition in northern Europe.

# The Land: The Geography, Climate, and Wildlife of Germany

A gray wolf roams the Bavarian Forest National Park. Due to hunting, wolf populations in Germany have decreased dramatically since the nineteenth century, but their numbers are beginning to rebound with government protection.

In the Alps, above the tree line, herds of wild goats and chamois—mountain antelope—range freely. Below the tree line are colonies of squirrel-like marmots. The snow hare, so called because its fur is snowy white in winter, is also common in the Alpine region. Badgers, which once thrived in all the wetlands of the country, had been hunted almost to extinction. Today they have returned to the rivers of eastern Germany. Near those rivers are small herds of elk and packs of wolves. The northern seacoast harbors seals, otters, and a great variety of waterfowl: storks, geese, cranes, sea eagles, sandpipers, and ducks. Many of the birds migrate from Africa across the Mediterranean Sea to feed on the fish of the North and Baltic Seas. Those fish include herring, flounder, cod, and perch.

Apart from fish and forests, Germany has few natural resources. Those it possesses in greatest quantity are hard coal, or anthracite, and brown coal, also called lignite. The hard coal is mined in the west, along the northern Rhine and in Saarland. Lignite, which is a lower-quality form of coal, is found in the Rhine and Leipzig basins and in Lower Lusatia along the Polish border. Germany also has iron ore in some of its mountains, small amounts of rock salt and potash (a potassium-based fertilizer derived from wood ash), and some oil and natural gas.

These few resources are not what have made Germany wealthy and strong. Even the beautiful scenery has not brought great strength or prosperity to the country. What has made Germany great is not its majestic mountains, its castled rivers, or its pleasant climate. Germany's greatness comes from its most valuable resource: its people.

A miner in Saarland oversees the extraction of coal from a mine. Saarland's vast coal fields once supported a large iron and steel industry, which is now in decline.

# THE PEOPLE

## 2

## From the Early Germanic Tribes to the Federal Republic of Germany

**H**uman history in Germany can be traced to the Stone Age. The skeletons of *Homo erectus* (which lived from 400,000 to 2 million years ago), Neanderthals (which lived from 30,000 to 300,000 years ago), and early *Homo sapiens* (our species, which first appeared 300,000 to 400,000 years ago) have all been found in Germany. About 4500 BC, Stone Age hunter-gatherers living within present-day Germany encountered people from southwest Asia who had moved into the Danube valley. The two groups intermarried and began farming and raising livestock.

During the Bronze Age, which began around 2500 BC in central Europe, new groups poured in. From modern-day Spain and Portugal to the west came the Bell-Beaker people, who had learned to fashion metal into tools. From somewhere near modern-day southern Russia to the east came the Battle-Axe tribes that settled around the Baltic Sea, in what are today Denmark, southern Norway, and south-western Sweden.

At left, a woman in traditional dress participates in a festival in Bavaria. Celebrants often wear their regional costumes at local fairs, parades, and festivals. Above are examples of early Germanic jewelry that date from the sixth century BC. These clasps and buckles are made of gold and silver and set with garnets.

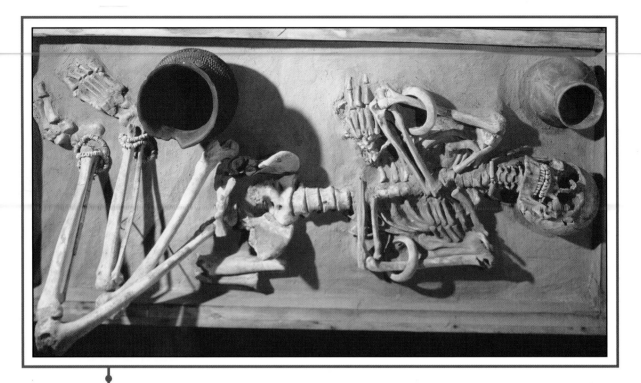

In the late nineteenth century, skeletal remains from the Neolithic age were found in Rössen, in Thuringia. This skeleton from the excavation site provides scientists with some clues about the burial rituals, religious traditions, and decorative pottery-making skills of the so-called Rössen culture.

## Early Peoples

Each Germanic tribe formed its own distinct kingdom. They fought one another for the most desirable living space. Some tribes formed alliances to fight against other tribes. These alliances often broke down, and former friends became foes. Eventually the Baltic tribes needed more room. In about 500 BC, they began moving to the south, displacing many Celtic peoples (the groups that would ultimately settle in Ireland, England, Scotland, Wales, and Brittany in France). By 100 BC, the Baltic tribes had fought their way into northern and central Germany as far as the Danube River. This brought them into contact with the Roman Empire, which was in the process of enlarging its domain based in present-day Italy.

The Romans considered the northern tribesmen to be fierce warriors. One of the tribes—the Tungri—called themselves Germani, and this name was eventually applied to many of the tribes and peoples of this area. When the warlike tribes entered Roman territory, the Roman emperor Caesar mustered his armies. The first battles were victories for the well-organized Romans, and some of the tribes made peace with Caesar and even joined his legions.

This early painting depicts wandering Germanic tribes at the time of the decline of the Roman Empire. Early Germanic tribes were described by the Romans as "barbarians." They were later given the name "Germanicus" to differentiate them from the Celts.

When Rome attempted to extend its rule into their territory, however, some of the Germanic tribes rebelled. Previously, Rome had conquered Gaul (present-day France) and established the Rhine as the boundary between its empire and the realms of the German peoples. In the first century AD, three Roman legions crossed that line. A prince of the Cherusci tribe, Arminius, knew the battle strategies of the Roman legions because he had served in the Roman army. In an event the Germans mark as the beginning of their history, Arminius defeated all three Roman legions in the Battle of Teutoburg Forest (AD 9). He forced the Romans beyond the Rhine back into Gaul.

For the next 400 years, Germans and Romans clashed repeatedly. But in the fourth and fifth centuries, a new force emerged that transformed all of Europe. The Huns, a barbaric tribe from central Asia, marched westward, conquering lands and killing people as they swept across the continent. Terrified Germans fled west and south. By the time Roman and German soldiers defeated the Hun's leader, Attila, in 451, the Roman Empire was completely shattered and Germanic peoples were

This colored engraving depicts Arminius, a first century AD chief of the Cherusci tribe. Under his military leadership, the Germans killed 20,000 Romans in Teutoburg Forest. The occupying Romans fled Germany and never again established a permanent settlement there.

This painting depicts the battle of Tolbaic in AD 496. Clovis I, king of the Franks (on horseback) is seen leading his tribesmen to victory over the Alemanni.

dispersed as far as modern-day Spain and the islands of Great Britain. Various German tribes have lent their names to places along their migration route: Saxony (the Saxons), Swabia (the Suebi), Franconia (the Franks) in Germany; Lombardy in Italy (the Lombards); Burgundy in France (the Burgundians); France itself (the Franks), and England (the Angles).

## Clovis and the Coming of Christianity

The area west of the Rhine, which the Romans had called Gaul, was now settled by Frankish tribes. Gradually the chief of the Salian Franks, Clovis, conquered many of the other tribal families living there. He declared himself king of the Franks in 486. Clovis continued to attack other tribes, trying to ram his way across the Rhine to absorb other German groups and control more territory.

At this time, the Germanic tribes were mostly pagan, meaning they believed in many gods, many of which were closely associated with nature. The Roman Empire, itself once pagan, had adopted Christianity in the fourth century. The Christian faith spread into Europe along with the Roman legions. In this transitional time, some family members might have converted to Christianity while others remained pagan. So, while Clovis's wife was a Christian, he continued to practice his tribe's older religion.

According to legend, Clovis, finding himself about to lose a battle, cried out to his wife's God for help, promising that he would become a Christian if he won. When he emerged victorious, the king and 3,000 of his soldiers received Christian baptism. Christianity gave Clovis a new cause to fight for and a new tool for uniting his subjects. He forced everyone he conquered to accept Christianity. His conversion also began an alliance between the throne and the Catholic Church that was to shape much of Germany's history for the next thousand years.

The influence of the church became evident in the later years of the Merovingian dynasty of Clovis and his sons (the dynasty was named for an ancestor of Clovis). Because of fighting within the royal family, real power was no longer exercised by the kings but by the mayors of the palace. In 751, the mayor Pepin the Short gained the favor of the pope, the head of the Roman Catholic Church based in Rome. With the pope's support, Pepin removed the king from power and imprisoned him. Pepin then arranged his own election as the ruler of the Franks. He and his descendants formed what became known as the Carolingian dynasty, named after later kings named Charles.

## The First Reich (800–1806)

The greatest of the Carolingian kings was Charlemagne, Pepin's son. Like Clovis and Pepin, he continued to fight wars designed to gain more territory and power. He fought the Slavs south of the Danube, conquered the Lombards in Italy, defeated the Saxons far east of the Rhine, and added parts of Bavaria to his kingdom. He protected the new state in Rome that his father had given to the church. A grateful Pope Leo III hailed Charlemagne as the champion of Christianity. On Christmas Day in the

This medieval manuscript depicts Emperor Charlemagne and his wife. After reuniting the Frankish kingdom, he became the first leader to be crowned emperor by the pope since Romulus Augustus in 476.

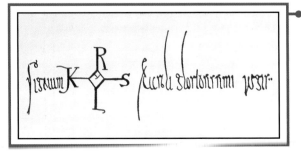

year 800, the pope crowned Charlemagne emperor of the Romans. He was given the title Kaiser, German for "Caesar."

After the deaths of Charlemagne and his son, the large kingdom was divided among Charlemagne's grandsons. The part called West Francia became modern-day France. East Francia evolved into today's Germany. By treaty, the ruler of East Francia retained the title of emperor of the Romans. In the thirteenth century, the official name of East Francia became the Holy Roman Empire, and in the fifteenth century it became the Holy Roman Empire of the German Nation.

Throughout the Middle Ages (fifth to the fifteenth centuries), Germany was ruled by a succession of dynasties: Saxon, Salian, Hohenstaufen, and Hapsburg (also known as Habsburg). German tribesmen elected their king, but they often chose weak kings who would not try to take away the nobles' local power. This practice kept Germany from being united under a central leader. Real power was in the hands of the king's officials (counts and military governors called margraves) and the tribes' military leaders (dukes). The German Reich, or government, was an empire in name only. In reality it was an association of independent states, each with its own prince or elector, that sometimes joined together for common causes and sometimes fought one another.

## German Disunity

Other factors added to German disunity. One was the involvement of the church in political affairs. The bishops owned large estates, which

This Roman amphitheater is found in Trier, Germany's oldest city. Trier was founded in 16 BC and was declared the regional capital by the Roman emperor Augustus.

gave them as much power as any other noble. They were princes of their own states, called bishoprics. The pope also flexed his political muscle in Germany. The princes elected the emperors, but the pope approved and crowned them. Great power struggles between the throne and the church kept the princes at odds with one another.

A second power struggle began in the thirteenth century. By this time, the German population had grown and the fiefs (estates) of the nobles were not large enough for all the people. The citizens who could find no other place to live and work began to join together and build cities that were not under the direct control of the lords and paid them no taxes or fees. They made their living in the new cities by trading goods. Several cities joined together in leagues to protect themselves and their interests from the greedy princes who were threatened by the citizens' growing independence and wealth. The largest of these leagues, the Hanseatic League, at one time included more than eighty-five cities. It was big enough, strong enough, and wealthy enough to place great political pressure on the king.

The primary obstacle to unification, however, was the ambition of the princes of the 240 states of the empire. Each one wanted to expand his own holdings. Each ruler's vision for a united Germany featured only himself on the throne, with all other princes defeated. As long as the German princes fought each other and the leaders of neighboring nations, Germany would never be unified under a single strong ruler.

Partly because Germany was being held back by its warring princes and was divided by violent religious disagreements (see Chapter 6), France had become the most powerful nation in Europe by the end of the eighteenth century. Its emperor, Napoléon Bonaparte, had marched across most of Europe and beyond, including invasions of Italy, Germany, Austria, Belgium, Spain, Russia, Syria, and Egypt. At this time, the Holy Roman Empire was now ruled by the Hapsburgs, princes of the German state of Austria. Napoléon invaded Germany in an attempt to add to his long list of official titles that of Holy Roman emperor. To prevent France from achieving this goal, the Hapsburg ruler Francis II dissolved the empire in 1806 and proclaimed himself simply emperor of Austria. Germany's First Reich had come to a sudden and quiet end.

## The Second Reich (1871–1918)

Napoléon was defeated in 1815 by a coalition of British, Russian, Prussian, Swedish, and Austrian forces. In the Congress of Vienna that followed Napoléon's defeat, the victorious powers divided the land France had won during his reign. As a result, several of the smaller German states were absorbed into larger ones. Now, instead of 240 principalities, there were only thirty-nine.

The new configuration was called the German Confederation. Each state in the confederation was still ruled by its nobles rather than leaders chosen directly by the people.

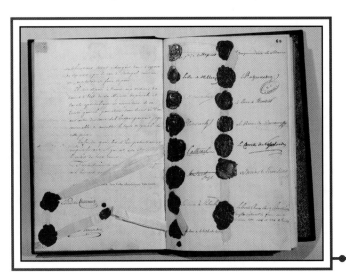

This document is the Final Act of the Congress of Vienna signed on June 9, 1815. Following Napoléon's defeat at Waterloo, this treaty established peace between France and the Allied nations of Europe.

The winds of revolution that had swept through most of western Europe and the New World had largely missed Germany. Throughout the continent and across the sea in North America, rule by the few had been replaced with constitutional governments in which a nation's citizens chose people to represent them in democratic government. In Germany, however, each of the princes and dukes of the thirty-nine principalities continued to cling to the dream of seizing sole control over all of Germany. One finally succeeded.

This nineteenth-century engraving depicts the Congress of Vienna. Negotiators from France, Great Britain, Prussia, Russia, and Austria are seen negotiating the peace treaty.

Otto von Bismarck, the prime minister of Prussia (an independent kingdom comprising parts of modern-day eastern Germany and northern Poland), represented King Wilhelm I in the German Confederation. Bismarck strongly opposed the idea of giving common people a voice in government, believing instead in a strong military and a single, powerful ruler for all the German states. He believed the great questions of the

Otto von Bismarck sits with two of his beloved Great Danes. He once said, "Our German forefathers . . . believed that, after death, they would meet again all the good dogs that had been their companions in life."

day could be settled not "by speeches and majority decisions . . . but by blood and iron." This earned Bismarck the nickname the Iron Chancellor.

Through a series of treaties and wars, Bismarck succeeded in enlarging Prussia, taking Schleswig-Holstein from Denmark, and capturing Austria-Hungary. By 1871, Prussia was strong enough for Bismarck to proclaim Wilhelm I the kaiser of the German Empire. For the first time in its history, Germany was united under one ruler. The Second Reich was born.

The Second Reich was powerful enough to spread fear throughout the other nations of Europe. It was larger than most of its European neighbors. It was also wealthier, having surpassed other countries in industrial production. Its iron and coal resources gave it an edge in making steel, machinery, railroads, and ships. Germany was aggressive, establishing colonies in Africa and building a mighty navy. The fear and mistrust Germany inspired led to a web of European alliances. Some European nations thought it best to remain on Germany's good side, while others banded together to defend themselves against Bismarck's aggression. These alliances split Europe into two heavily armed camps.

This uneasy peace was broken on June 28, 1914, when Archduke Franz Ferdinand, heir to the Austro-Hungarian throne, was assassinated by a Serbian nationalist who desired Serb independence from the Austro-Hungarian Empire. Austria-Hungary responded to the assassination by cracking down on the Serbian nationalist movement, which angered Russia, a Serbian ally. What followed was a gradual worsening of the crisis that drew more and more of Europe into the fray. The delicate system of shifting European alliances created by German aggression

This 1916 photograph shows German soldiers positioned in a trench during World War I. After the invention of the machine gun and heavy artillery limited soldiers' mobility on the battlefield, the battles of World War I were often fought in networks of trenches.

eventually led thirty-two nations, including the United States and Canada, into what later became known as the Great War, or World War I (1914–1918).

After four long years of brutal and bloody trench warfare, Germany and its allies were defeated by the Allied forces of France, Great Britain, the United States, Canada, and several other nations. Kaiser Wilhelm II gave up his throne and Germany became a republic in 1918. This new German government was known as the Weimar Republic, named after the city in which the nation's new constitution was created following the war.

## The Third Reich (1933–1945)

The time of the Weimar Republic was difficult for Germany. The victors of World War I had imposed extremely harsh penalties on Germany. Because Germany had been the first to declare war, the winners forced it to accept blame for causing the war and full responsibility for paying for it. The nation was forbidden to have a navy and any defensive force except for a tiny volunteer army. Germany was crushed physically, politically, financially, and psychologically. The worldwide Depression of the early 1930s made already difficult conditions absolutely desperate.

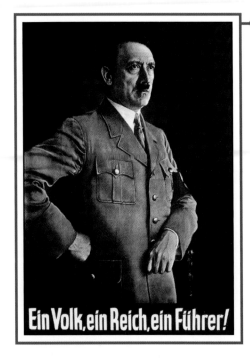

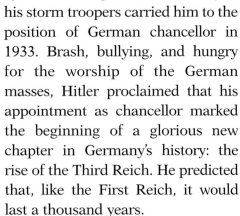

This propaganda poster from Nazi-era Germany depicts Adolf Hitler and the slogan, "One People, One Country, One Leader!" Before coming to power, Hitler won public attention by giving many speeches in beer halls and town squares, appealing to the average German's sense of nationalism and grievance.

Into this bleak situation marched what appeared to be a savior to many impoverished and humiliated Germans. Adolf Hitler, a failed artist and embittered veteran of World War I, rose out of nowhere to become head of the Nazi Party, a group dedicated to German nationalism and national and racial "purity." Hitler rallied the suffering citizens with stirring speeches about the supremacy of the German people. He gave them a scapegoat for all the guilt and misery resulting from World War I, telling them the Jews were to blame. And he amassed his own private army of more than 400,000 storm troopers. The popularity of his message and the brutality of his storm troopers carried him to the position of German chancellor in 1933. Brash, bullying, and hungry for the worship of the German masses, Hitler proclaimed that his appointment as chancellor marked the beginning of a glorious new chapter in Germany's history: the rise of the Third Reich. He predicted that, like the First Reich, it would last a thousand years.

This photograph shows skeletal Holocaust victims at the Buchenwald concentration camp. Eventual Nobel Prize–winning author Elie Wiesel can be seen in the second bunk from the bottom, sixth from left.

But Hitler's dream of presiding over a revived and legendary German Empire was to last only twelve horrific years. In that brief span, he plunged the entire world into a second catastrophic war that again destroyed most of the country. During the war, more than 30 million civilians and 24 million soldiers on both sides were killed. Included in this grim figure are the 6 million Eastern European Jews and 5 to 6 million non-Jews (including Catholics, Gypsies, homosexuals, and prisoners of war) exterminated in the concentration camps Hitler and his Nazi henchmen designed, built, and operated throughout Europe. Ninety percent of the Jews of Germany were murdered by the Nazis. As the American, French, British, Canadian, and Soviet Allies closed in on Berlin and Germany's impending defeat became obvious to him, Hitler committed suicide. With Hitler's death and Germany's defeat, both the Third Reich and the brief seventy-four-year history of a unified Germany also came to an end.

## A Germany Divided

World War II's four most powerful victors—the Allied powers of the United States, Britain, France, and the Soviet Union—divided Germany into four zones. Each country took responsibility for administering one of these zones. The Allies wanted to avoid the mistakes of the aftermath of World War I—when Germany was humiliated and impoverished by the terms of the peace treaty—and instead rebuild the political and economic structures of Germany so it could become a strong, responsible, stable, and peaceful member of the European community.

Almost immediately, however, a number of differences arose among the three western Allied powers and the Soviet Union. Afraid that the Communist

A soldier raises the Soviet flag from Germany's parliament building—the Reichstag—in Berlin in 1945 soon after Adolf Hitler's suicide and the Allied defeat of Germany in World War II.

East German soldiers begin to construct the Berlin wall in August 1961. The sign at the right marks the border between Communist East Germany and democratic West Germany.

Soviet Union might try to take over more of Germany in its quest to dominate Eastern Europe, the western occupiers joined their areas into a single zone. As a result, in 1949, the western and eastern zones became two distinct countries. The Federal Republic of Germany (West Germany) was democratic; the German Democratic Republic (East Germany) was Communist. The city of Berlin, located in East Germany, was divided in half. The western half now belonged to the Federal Republic, while the eastern half belonged to the Democratic Republic.

Neither of the two Germanys would give up the hope of someday reunifying the country. West Germany refused to draft a constitution, claiming that the divided state was a temporary condition. Instead, the government wrote a Basic Law that was to be followed in West Germany until it was reunited with East Germany. Many in East Germany also wanted reunification, but their Communist government closed the country's borders, preventing people from going in or out. In 1953, East Germans protested their lack of freedom and the heavy work demands placed upon them. This "people's uprising" was crushed by Soviet tanks. In that year alone, 330,000 East Germans illegally

A citizen of West Germany looks out over the Berlin wall from the French section of the city. After the wall went up, 10,000 East Germans tried to escape over, under, or through it.

fled to West Germany. By 1961, almost 3 million people had risked their lives to escape East Germany.

The exodus of so much of its workforce created a crisis for East Germany. Its response was to wall its people in. East Germany fenced and mined its entire border with the west. The city of Berlin, however, remained a trouble spot. The Communist government's solution to this problem came on the night of August 12, 1961, when East Berlin began to be sealed off from West Berlin by what would become a 102-mile (165 km) wall of concrete. On the eastern side was a no-man's-land of barbed wire and land mines patrolled by armed guards and attack dogs. From 1961 to 1989, more than 100 people died trying to climb over the wall to the west.

Germans separated from some of their friends and relatives for over twenty years swarm toward the Berlin wall as the border separating the two Germanys is again opened. On November 9, 1989, travel restrictions were lifted and 10,000 East Germans entered West Berlin. Over the following weeks, the wall was torn down, piece by piece.

## Reunified Germany

West Germany stubbornly refused to recognize that East Germany was an independent country, clinging to the conviction that the two would be one again. That goal was not achieved by West German efforts, but by the disintegration of the Soviet

Union, which had wielded enormous power and influence over the Communist nations of Eastern Europe. Beginning in the late 1980s, people throughout Eastern Europe rose up and shook themselves free of Soviet control and their own Communist leaders.

On November 9, 1989, East Germany removed all travel restrictions, and its citizens removed the most hated and feared symbol of those restrictions—the Berlin wall. With a few swings of sledgehammers, the wall was breached and East Germans and West Germans suddenly found themselves embracing and celebrating together in the streets of a unified Berlin.

From that moment, no one questioned the fact that the two Germanys would be reunited. That task, however, was immensely difficult. During their forty years of separation, the two countries had developed very differently. They had completely different political structures, economic practices, currencies, social systems, educational systems, and standards of living. For example, wages in East Germany were one-third of what they were in West Germany.

Reunification was achieved gradually and very carefully. Economic reunification began on July 1, 1990, with East Germany accepting West Germany's deutsche mark (DM) as its official currency. Political reunification occurred on October 3, 1990, when the Basic Law adopted by the West in 1949 was accepted by the East as the constitution for the unified Federal Republic of Germany. Education was not unified until 1994.

Reunification made Germany more than a geographic bridge between east and west, but a cultural bridge as well. The new Germany established cooperative ties with nations on both sides of the Cold War divide. It was a major force in bringing formerly Communist Eastern European nations into the Western alliances of NATO (North Atlantic Treaty Organization, a military alliance) and the European Union (EU). Reunification also reestablished Germany as the nation at the geographical, political, and financial heart of Europe.

## The Germans

The reunified Germany contains 83 million people. Ethnic Germans belong to one of two Caucasian groups: Alpine (mostly in the south and central regions) and Teutonic (largely in the north). The first-century Roman historian Tacitus described the Teutons as having "eyes stern and blue, yellow hair, huge bodies." The Alpine Germans, having mixed with the Romans, have darker eyes and hair.

Because the German states that evolved from the various tribes remained independent and separate from each other for so long, some differences can still be seen among people in different regions of the country. Each region often has distinct dialects, traditions, and characteristics. For example, residents of Mecklenburg in northeastern Germany are considered particularly reserved. The Swabians in the south are said to be careful with their money. Those along the northern Rhine are thought to be easygoing and carefree, unlike the Saxons, who are considered serious, hardworking people.

A mother and her son play outside near their home in Bobrach, in the Bavarian forest. Many Bavarians tend to be very tradition-minded and devoutly Catholic. Bavaria, which is largely covered by forests, fields, and small villages, has one of the lowest unemployment rates in the country.

## Minorities

Three minority groups have lived in Germany for many centuries. Each has its own language and culture. The largest is a Slavic group known as the Sorbs or the Wends. They settled east of the Elbe and Saale Rivers in the sixth century. About 120,000 Sorbs live

A German girl shares a haystack with her pet dog. Traditionally, dogs have been favorite pets with Germans and are treated almost like equal members of the family.

in Brandenburg and Saxony today. They keep their language and culture strong through schools, associations, and the Institute of Sorbian Studies at the University of Leipzig.

A Danish minority of about 60,000 lives in Schleswig-Holstein, near Denmark. This group also has its own schools, churches, libraries, and other institutions. The Danish political party is strong enough to maintain at least one representative in the state government.

In addition, a small minority of about 12,000 Frisians lives on the Frisian Islands and the North Sea coast. The Frisian language is closely related to Dutch.

Two Gypsy groups make up a third minority in Germany: the Sinti and the Roma. The Sinti have lived in Germany for hundreds of years, but many of the Roma first arrived from Romania after the 1989 overthrow of its Communist government. The population of these two groups in Germany has been as high as 70,000, but some of the Romas have begun returning to Romania.

## Foreigners

Members of the minority groups described above are all German citizens. About 9 percent of the country's population consists of foreigners who are not citizens. One large wave of immigrants came in the 1950s, when West Germany invited "guest workers" from Italy, Greece, Yugoslavia, Portugal, Spain, Morocco, Tunisia, and Turkey to help

A group of Turkish Muslim women waits for a subway at an underground station in Berlin. Turkish immigrants—numbering almost 2.5 million—make up the largest immigrant group living in Germany.

reconstruct what World War II had shattered. The foreign workers then settled in the country they helped rebuild.

A second group of foreigners arrived after the collapse of Communism in the 1990s. Some had been expelled from Germany under Nazi rule. Others were refugees from the countries of the former Soviet Union, eager to share in the prosperity of the west. Any repatriates (people coming back to their home country) who could show they had German blood and could speak German automatically became German citizens.

Germany also welcomes immigrants who claim they are persecuted in their own countries and would risk death by returning home. They ask for asylum, or political protection. Because so many Germans and other Europeans were persecuted during the Nazi era, Germany has adopted a more liberal policy for asylum seekers than any other nation. Today about 100,000 people come to Germany every year claiming they are fleeing persecution. About 7 percent of them are allowed to stay.

This great variety of people—whether Teuton, Alpine, Gypsy, Dane, citizen, or immigrant—shares at least one thing in common: language. Ninety-nine percent of the German population over the age of fifteen can speak, read, and write German. This is what draws the people together and helps soften the differences of ethnicity, custom, appearance, and income. More than any dictator has been able to do in Germany's long history, the common language used by its citizens provides the true unity of this newly reunified nation.

# THE GERMAN LANGUAGE

## 3

German is the first language of nearly 100 million people in more than twenty countries. It is the official language of Germany and Austria and one of the official languages of Switzerland. German is an Indo-European language, which means it is one of the family of Indian and European languages that evolved from a common prehistoric language. Other Indo-European languages include Kashmiri, Hindi, Persian, Greek, Russian, Polish, the Scandinavian languages, Dutch, English, Spanish, French, Italian, and the Gaelic languages of Ireland, Scotland, Wales, and Brittany.

Sometime before the eighth century, people in the higher altitudes of Germany began pronouncing their consonants differently from their lower altitude neighbors. This sound shift led to a division of the language into High German and Low German. High German was further divided into Upper and Middle. The names came from the regions in which they were spoken: High German in the high-elevation southern and central highlands, Middle German in the central uplands, and Low German in the lowland regions of the north. Numerous dialects (regional variations of a language) of all three branches are still spoken in Germany today.

Most of the differences in German dialects involve pronunciation and grammar rather than vocabulary, but some of the regional words and phrases are so different that people in one area have difficulty understanding those in another.

Hans Werner Kilz is the editor in chief of German newspaper *Suddeutsche Zeitung* in Munich. *Süddeutsche Zeitung* is a national paper and is widely read all over Germany. Above: Schoolchildren learn the proper spellings of German words by using a dictionary to do their homework.

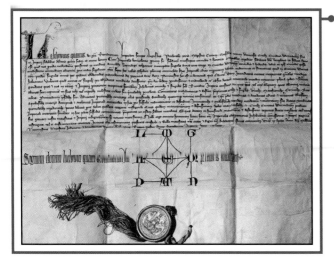

An official letter bears the seal of Louis IV, the Holy Roman Emperor from 1314 to 1347.

## History of the German Language

The nation's many emerging dialects can be seen in the earliest German writings, which date from about 750. Even when the various tribes and regions became loosely united in the Holy Roman Empire, no single dialect prevailed. The language the empire used in official documents was Latin, the language of the first Roman Empire and the language of the Catholic Church.

The late medieval emperor Louis "the Bavarian" IV (1282–1347) clashed so strongly with the pope that the pope excommunicated him from (kicked him out of) the church. Louis then declared that court documents would no longer be written in Latin, but in German. Over the next century and a half, several of the German states adopted dialects of Middle High German for their official writings. By 1500, German was the language of the Universities of Leipzig and Wittenberg and of the courts throughout Saxony and Thuringia. It had replaced Latin as the written language of the educated.

At this time, differences among regional dialects still made communication among Germans somewhat difficult. The language began to become standardized in 1532, when Martin Luther (founder of the Protestant movement) translated the Bible into German. Luther, a native of Saxony, chose the Saxon dialect for his translation. In addition to translating the Bible, Luther wrote hymns, catechisms (teaching manuals), pamphlets, and books—all in High German. Other writers followed Luther's lead, using the same form of the language. By 1600, High German was the literary language of the German-speaking people.

Even with growing agreement upon a standard literary or official language, the language used for more everyday purposes was still written differently in various parts of the country. In the nineteenth century, Jacob and Wilhelm Grimm—the famous folklorists who compiled many German folk and fairy tales—published the first part of a dictionary of the German language. This helped standardize the spelling of words.

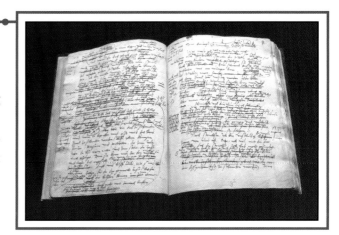

This is a 1530 handwritten translation of the Bible from Latin into German by Martin Luther. The manuscript was later sent to a printer to be made into printed bibles.

In 1901, a uniform system for writing the language was accepted by scholars. Attempts have also been made to outline a standard for pronunciation, but so far none have been successful.

## Features of the German Language

German is an inflected language. This means that different endings are added to words to show who is speaking or being spoken to, the gender (male or female) of the speaker or listener, and the purpose of the sentence (question, command, statement). The ending of a verb might indicate person (I, you, he), tense (present, past, future), number, or mood. For example, the endings of the word for "come" change depending on whether I am coming *(ich komme)*, you are coming *(Sie kommen)*, or he is coming *(er kommt)*.

Just as word endings are important, prefixes also make the meanings of German words more precise. Consider the verb *führen*, which means "to lead." Adding *aus* (out) to the beginning produces the German word for "execute" or "carry out." The prefix *ein* (in) produces "introduce." Adding *auf* (on) makes it "to perform on a stage."

Every noun in German has a gender—masculine, feminine, or neuter—and the adjectives and articles that go with them must have the same gender. So the word similar to the English article "the" changes according to the gender of the noun: the

This nineteenth-century engraving depicts Jacob Ludwig Carl Grimm *(right)* and Wilhelm Carl Grimm *(seated)*, the famous compilers of German folk and fairy tales.

A student practices German spelling and grammar at school. German students are held to high academic standards.

church (feminine) is *die Kirche,* its steeple (masculine) is *der Turm,* and its gate (neuter) is *das Tor.* A peculiarity of German writing that can be seen in these examples is that nouns are always capitalized.

Many German nouns are familiar to the English speaker because the earliest form of English was closely related to German and brought to England by migrating Anglo-Saxons. Some words are perfect cognates—their meanings and spellings are the same in both languages. Others are near cognates, with very similar spellings. Still others are English words that have been incorporated into German with little or no change.

Even when German and English words are spelled the same, they may be pronounced differently. In German, the *w* has a *v* sound, and the *v* is pronounced like an *f. Th* is said as though the *h* were not there. When an *i* and an *e* are together, they make the sound of the second vowel rather than the first. Thus Weimar is pronounced VYE-mar and Wiesbaden is VEEZ-bah-den. The accent is always on the first syllable unless that syllable is a prefix.

Another interesting feature of German is its use of compound words—when two or more words are joined together to form a new word. "People's" *(Volks)* + "car" *(Wagen)* is *Volkswagen*; "people's" + "mouth" *(Mund)* is *Volksmund,* the everyday language of common people. A *Wörterbuch* ("word" + "book") is a dictionary. The word for "animal" is *Tier,* and a skunk is a *Stinktier.*

## Non-German Languages

Although nearly everyone in Germany speaks German, a number of people use other languages in most of their daily lives. Each of the four national minorities—Sorbs, Danes, Frisians, and Sinti and Roma—has its own language. These languages are officially recognized by the government.

The Sorbs, or Wends, have had difficulty preserving their language. Throughout the Middle Ages, stronger tribes tried to Germanize this Slavic group.

The language was banned in the thirteenth, seventeenth, and twentieth centuries, but it managed to survive. Of the many original Sorb dialects, two are still spoken today. They are sometimes classified as two different languages: Upper Sorbian and Lower Sorbian. As with German, the two languages can be further broken down by regional dialects. These are Slavic languages, similar to Polish and Czech.

In a few cities where the Sorbian population is large, schools use the Lusatian languages exclusively. In other cities, the language is taught as an academic subject and second language. Some newspapers and magazines are published in Sorbian, and the language is studied at the Sorbian Institute in Bautzen and the Institute for Sorbian Studies at the University of Leipzig. At least 70,000 people speak it today.

Fewer Germans speak Danish, perhaps 40,000. Most German Danish-speakers live near the edge of Denmark, and many use their Danish in cross-border business dealings. Danish is an Indo-European, Germanic language, but it developed separately from German. It is from the East Scandinavian family of languages. In northern Germany today, Danish is the language of instruction in more than fifty schools. It is used in 70 percent of the articles in the newspaper *Flensborg Avis*, which is read by 6,000 people. The Danish minority maintains its language through local newscasts, theater groups, and cultural activities.

The Danish newspaper includes articles in another minority language: Frisian. Two varieties of Frisian are spoken in Germany. Sater Frisian, or Seeltersk, is heard among the 2,000 Frisians living in three villages in Lower Saxony. Nine dialects of North Frisian, or Friisk, are spoken by 8,000 people in the Frisian Islands and in rural areas along the coast of the North Sea. It is a Germanic language closely related to Dutch and, to a lesser extent, English.

The fourth minority language is Romany, spoken by the Gypsy groups the Sinti and Roma. These traveling people have lived in Germany for generations. They do not live in one specific area as the other minorities do. Instead, their communities are scattered throughout the entire country, and they often move around. Their language is Indo-European but not Germanic. The language and the people probably originated in northern India.

No matter what his or her first language is, every German speaks German. Most Germans speak a second language as well. The most common second language is English. German is the tongue of culture and learning, but English is the language of commerce.

Kinder- und Hausmärchen

gesammelt

durch die

Brüder Grimm

Berlin, Ferd. Dümmlers Verlagsbuchhandlung.

# GERMAN MYTHS AND LEGENDS

4

L ong before the German tribes created a written language, they kept memories of the past alive through stories and songs. Told and retold as the different tribes interacted and scattered, the tales were carried far and wide. Details often changed with each new telling, so that various versions of the same story were carried by migrating tribes throughout Germany, Scandinavia, and Iceland. Some of these tales were finally written down beginning in the ninth century.

A legend is a story that has some basis in fact. The German legends spring from events of the second to the sixth centuries, when the various tribes were wandering throughout northern Europe. Exaggerated and impossible exploits were attributed to the heroes of those times. In the stories, some of the historical characters appear next to others who actually lived generations later. The real-life deeds of one person were often attributed to another. Facts were distorted to further boost the heroes' reputations. The most popular of the German legends are the Dietrich saga and the *Nibelungenlied.*

## Dietrich Saga

Dietrich is the High German name for Theodoric the Great, a fifth-century king of the Ostrogoths (a Germanic tribe). In the legend, Dietrich's evil uncle captured some of Dietrich's knights and demanded his kingdom as ransom

At left is an 1885 cover illustration from a collection of fairy tales collected and written by the Grimm brothers. The title can be translated as "Children's and Household Tales." One of the tales collected by the Grimm brothers was "The Pied Piper of Hameln," about a piper who is not paid by a village for his help in ridding it of rats. As revenge, he lures all the village's children away, and they are never heard from again. A re-creation of the tale is taking place above.

for the knights' lives. Exiled, Dietrich lived at the court of Attila the Hun for thirty years. In that time, he gathered an army of Huns and returned to claim what was his. Dietrich defeated his uncle in a bloody battle and was restored to his rightful lands and position.

This is the basic outline of the Dietrich saga. Admirers of the king filled in this historical episode with fanciful tales of the daring adventures of Dietrich and his men. In these highly fictional versions of the story, Dietrich rescues maidens and knights, slaughters evil and powerful enemies, and successfully battles giants, dwarfs, and dragons.

## Nibelungenlied

The *Nibelungenlied* (Song of the Nibelungs) is the best known of all German legends. Like the Dietrich saga, it is rooted in ancient times. Unlike the stories of Dietrich, which survive only in scattered episodes, thirteenth-century copies of the complete, long poem have been found. Versions of the story also appear in the Scandinavian *Volsungasaga* and the Icelandic *Edda*.

The *Nibelungenlied* has been called the great German epic. It is the story of the warrior Siegfried. He is the typical epic hero in that no one is stronger, more handsome, or braver than he. He kills two princes of the Nibelung family (members of the Burgundian tribe) and becomes lord of Nibelungland. He then seizes the Nibelungs' treasure and slays a dragon. As he bathes in the dragon's blood, his body becomes protected against any weapon. However, a tree's leaf falling on his back blocks the magic

This fifteenth-century manuscript illumination illustrates a scene from the *Nibelungenlied*. Kriemhild, a daughter of the king of Burgundy, arrives at the court of the pagan Etzel, king of the Huns.

blood from seeping into one small spot. This becomes Siegfried's only vulnerability.

After many daring deeds and larger-than-life adventures, Siegfried's enemy, Hagen, learns the secret of both Siegfried's strength and hidden weakness. In a cowardly act, Hagen murders Siegfried by striking him on the back in the exact spot left unprotected by the dragon's blood. Hagen then steals the treasure of the Nibelungs and buries it in a secret place in the Rhine River.

Siegfried's wife plots for many years and finally avenges her husband's death. In a gruesome battle that she arranges, nearly everyone on both sides is slaughtered. She slays Hagen and his accomplice with her own hands. She too is killed. The story ends by touching upon all the classic themes of German legend: heroic deeds, honor, betrayal, courage, revenge, and tragedy.

## Myths

While legends, no matter how exaggerated, have some basis in history, stories with no connection to historical fact are called myths. Myths are often told to account for some natural phenomenon, such as why the sun rises and sets, why the seasons change, or why the rain falls. Such is the case with the myths of the Rhine maidens, which were probably invented to warn against the dangerous rocks and tides of the deceptively beautiful river.

One Rhine maiden story centers on a cliff near the town of St. Goarshausen. Here the 400-foot-high (122 m) rock that rises from the river produces an echoing sound. Swift currents, low mists, and rocks hidden beneath the water's surface have claimed the lives of many a sailor below this cliff. Locals may have made up the tale, which was preserved when Klemens Bretano first published the story in 1800. It was made famous when Heinrich Heine told the tale in a poem he called "Lorelei."

The Lorelei Cliff is located on the Rhine near Saint Goarshausen. The cliff and the hidden rocks and turbulent tides below are thought to be the inspiration for the Lorelei legend.

According to the myth, Lorelei was a beautiful young maiden with long, golden hair. She loved a man who did not return her love. In despair, she threw herself off the cliff into the river. Now she sits on the rock and sings to all who sail near. Her song is beautiful and magically lures boatmen to the rocks below the cliff upon which they crash and drown.

## Folklore

Folklore is the traditional stories and sayings of a people. These are not tales of glory recited in the castles, but everyday stories of common folk. Folklore contains a culture's wisdom and humor, as well as the values and fears of its people.

Most Germanic folklore consists of fanciful stories of children, elves, witches, fairies, and talking animals. More than 200 of these stories were collected by Jacob and Wilhelm Grimm. The Grimm brothers were university professors. They wrote scholarly books on the history and grammar of the German language and serious discussions of German myths and literature. They spent years compiling the stories of the common people—stories like "Cinderella," "Hansel and Gretel," and "The Frog Prince." From

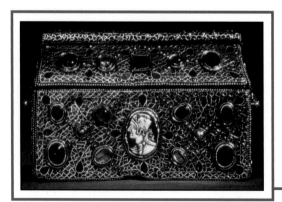

This is the bejeweled reliquary of Theodoric the Great (AD 455–528). He was the king of the Ostrogoths and conqueror of Italy. A reliquary is a container of bones or sacred objects associated with an important leader or religious figure.

# Lorelei

By Heinrich Heine, translated by Walter Meyer

I'm looking in vain for the reason
That I am so sad and distressed;
A tale known for many a season
Will not allow me to rest.

Cool is the air in the twilight
And quietly flows the Rhine;

The mountain top
glows with
   a highlight
From the evening sun's
   last shine.

The fairest of
   maiden's reposing
So wondrously
   up there.

Her golden treasure disclosing;
She's combing her golden hair.

She combs it with comb of gold
And meanwhile sings a song
With melody strangely bold
And overpoweringly strong.

The boatman in his small craft
Is seized with longings and sighs.
He sees not the rocks fore and aft;
He looks only up towards the skies.

I fear that the waves shall be flinging
Both vessel and man to their end;
That must have been what with
   her singing
The Lorelei did intend.

1812 to 1815, they published what they collected under the title *Household Tales.* The collection was later called *Grimm's Fairy Tales.*

The legends, myths, and folklore of Germany say much about the nation's culture and its people. They reveal a strong commitment to the heroic values of strength, courage, truth, and wisdom. The importance of family and community ties is repeatedly emphasized. And they reveal the richness of the German imagination, which is as dark and violent as it is humorous and fanciful.

A 1903 drawing by artist Alfred Zimmermann depicts the seven dwarfs discovering Snow White.

# GERMAN FESTIVALS AND CEREMONIES OF ANTIQUITY AND TODAY

**5**

G erman people love to celebrate. And with their long and colorful past, their rich culture, and their zest for life, they can find hundreds of reasons to make merry throughout the year. Their many celebrations revolve around music, food and drink, religious feasts, and local traditions.

## Music Festivals

As the birthplace of many of the world's most famous classical musicians, Germany is filled with song. Most Germans' favorite time for musical performances is when the regular indoor concert season ends and the large outdoor summer festivals begin. A number of cities host summer music festivals, but the ones held in Munich, Berlin, and Bayreuth are particularly large and well attended.

The Munich summer festivals showcase the old and the new. The Munich Opera Festival always features some of the most cherished and popular operas, while the Munich Biennal, a two-week event held every two years, features compositions of the late twentieth and the twenty-first centuries. The biennal has an international flavor, with works by composers from around the world, including India, Italy, China, and, of course, Germany.

At left, an Oktoberfest celebrant in traditional dress joins a parade in Munich. The original Munich Oktoberfest is the largest fair in the world. Many cities around the world now hold their own Oktoberfests. Above is a float from a Weinfest in Rhineland-Palatinate. Rhineland is the home of some of the world's most famous white wines.

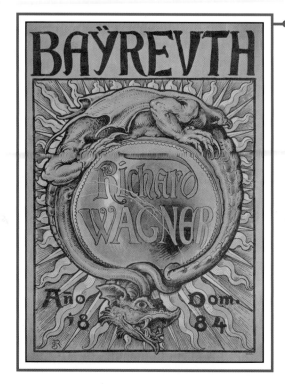

This 1884 program cover announces the eighth annual Bayreuth Festival, held a year after the death of the festival's founder, Richard Wagner.

The Berlin Festival Weeks have been a summer fixture since 1951. They began in the western part of the divided city as a cultural bridge between east and west. Their purpose was not to recall the famous works of Germany's past, but to unify all Germans around their shared love of the arts. In addition to music (including opera, jazz, and international music), festival weeks include drama, ballet, literature, art exhibitions, and a film festival.

The most lavish of the German summer performances is the monthlong Wagner Opera Festival in Bayreuth. It was begun by Richard Wagner, Germany's most celebrated opera composer, in 1876 and has been continued by the composer's descendants. Designed by Wagner to feature the work of other composers, today the festival presents nothing but Wagner's own operas. The theater in which the festival is held was designed by Wagner and built for him by King Ludwig of Bavaria. To keep the sound as pure as possible, Wagner insisted that the walls remain bare. In addition, the wooden seats have no padding or upholstery. Every evening of the festival, 1,900 people sit on the uncomfortable benches for the four- to five-hour performance. Women arrive in long evening gowns, and men must wear tuxedos and black ties. The festival is extremely popular, and no seat is ever empty. Tickets are very expensive and can only be obtained through a lottery system. It can take some opera fans years to finally get tickets to a festival performance.

## Food and Drink Festivals

While everyone may not be able to afford tickets to a music festival, food and drink parties are open to everyone in Germany. Hundreds of wine festivals are held each

A waitress serves another round of beer to visitors at one of Germany's beer festivals. Ancient Germans regarded beer as a sacrifice to the gods. They started producing the first alcoholic beer around 800 BC.

year in the wine-growing regions along the Rhine and Mosel Rivers. Most are held in September, during the harvesting season.

One of the largest of these exuberant events is the Wurstmarkt (Sausage Fair) of Bad Dürkheim. Begun in 1442, it is held around the feast of Saint Michael. More than 500,000 people from all over Europe come for the seven days of the festival.

While some cities celebrate their wines, others praise their beers. The most famous of the beer festivals is Munich's Oktoberfest, which actually begins in late September and ends on the first Sunday of October. Like many German festivals, it commemorates a historical event. It began in 1810 to celebrate the wedding of Princess Therese of Saxony to Bavarian Crown Prince Ludwig (who later became King Ludwig I). The entire city of Munich was invited to the royal party. Oktoberfest seeks to recreate the joy and festivity of that first party. Today's Oktoberfest draws more than 6 million celebrants each year. People in traditional Bavarian costumes perform folk dances to the music of oompah bands. Vendors sell sausages, pretzels, and, of course, beer. Parades, giant Ferris wheels, roller coasters, and other amusements keep people occupied for the sixteen days of the festival.

## Religious Celebrations

Germans seldom limit their celebrations to just one day. They turn holidays into season-long festivities. In the United States, the beginning of Lent (the forty days between Ash Wednesday and Easter Sunday) is observed with a single night of revelry—Fat Tuesday, or Mardi Gras. This is a final burst of celebration before the penance and fasting of Lent begin on Ash Wednesday. In Germany the pre-Lent feasting can last for months. The Karneval season—also called Fasnet, Fassenacht,

Fastnacht, and Fasching—begins at eleven minutes after eleven on the eleventh day of the eleventh month (November). It finally comes to an end on Ash Wednesday, which is usually in February or March. Karneval is a time of street parades, masquerade balls, and wild costumes.

Another type of costume is worn on Walpurgis Night, similar to our Halloween. Walpurgis Night is April 30, the eve of the feast of Saint Walpurga. In centuries past, peasants in the Harz Mountains believed that witches met with the devil on this night and flew off on broomsticks or goats. The peasants lit fires and hung crosses on their doors to protect themselves from the evil visitors. Today, people dress as witches and warlocks, light bonfires, and have parties.

Parties take place in many small communities of southern Germany on the anniversaries of the dedications of their churches. Originally religious observances of thanksgiving, these *Kirchweih* (church consecration) festivals have evolved into something like county fairs. Amusement rides, game booths, and traditional foods are all part of the event. Men in *lederhosen* (leather shorts) and women in folk costumes dance to the music of Bavarian brass bands.

## Christmas

Perhaps the largest religious celebration in Germany is Christmas. Christmas in Germany officially lasts an entire month, from December 6 (the Feast of Saint Nicholas) to January 6 (the Feast of the Three Kings). Both Christmas Day and the day after are national holidays. On the Feast of Saint Nicholas, children go to bed dreaming of Saint Nicholas with his long beard, tall bishop's hat, and staff. The German Saint Nicholas closely resembles the bishop-saint upon which our Santa Claus was

Saint Nicholas, or *Weihnachtsmann* (Father Christmas), pulls a sleigh full of toys and Christmas trees. In the rear of the sleigh sits the Christ Child (*Christkindl*).

Overjoyed German children open their gifts on Christmas Eve while their parents gaze at the Christmas tree (*Tannenbaum*) brightly lit by candles.

based. Saint Nicholas will come on a sled drawn by a donkey, and leave goodies in children's shoes. German children also receive presents on Christmas Eve. They are not brought by Saint Nicholas, but by *Christkindl*—the Christ Child.

The practice of bringing a pine tree indoors and decorating it for Christmas began in Germany. Several stories are told of how the custom may have started, but no one really knows for sure. Early Europeans believed in evil spirits, witches, ghosts, and trolls. As the winter solstice approached— December 21, the day of the year on which the sun is farthest from Earth in the Northern Hemisphere—many people feared the sun would never return and the days would forever remain short and dark.

Special rituals and celebrations were held to encourage the return of the sun. The pre-Christian Celts of Gaul and Britain brought evergreen plants into their homes at the time of the winter solstice, both to provide friendly spirits with a refuge and shelter against the harsh winter and to remind themselves of the green life that would return to the bleak land in the spring. This custom may have evolved into the German *Tannenbaum* (Christmas tree). However it began, the lights placed on the tree were originally candles, and Germans still prefer to use candles rather than electric lights on their holiday trees.

The Christmas season ends on January 6 with the Feast of the Three Kings. This commemorates the day the Three Wise Men are said to have paid their respects to the baby Jesus in the manger. On January 6, the current year and the initials of the three wise men are chalked over the doors of German homes. A prayer is said, asking God to watch over the house through the following year.

Young children in traditional dress prepare for the Kinderzeche Pageant in Bayern. The pageant, in which young children between the ages of three and twelve march and sing in a parade through the city, honors the turning back of Swedish forces by the children of the town of Dinkelsbühl.

## Local Festivals

Because Germany was divided into several principalities throughout much of its long history, each region developed special festivities of its own. Most of these local festivals stem from a historical event important to the area.

The Thirty Years' War (see chapter 6) was the inspiration for the *Kinderzeche* (children's reckoning) in Dinkelsbühl. In 1632, a Swedish colonel laid siege to the German town. Knowing they could not win a fight, the town council agonized over surrendering Dinkelsbühl. While the town's adults deliberated over what to do, the watchman's daughter gathered a group of children and stood before the enemy, singing. The Swedish colonel, whose own young son had recently died, was moved to pity by the children's singing and withdrew from the town. Ever since that day, a yearly pageant has been held to commemorate the town's rescue at the hands of children.

Another seemingly miraculous event is celebrated in the Bavarian village of Oberammergau.

Amateur actors from the town of Oberammergau re-create the final hours of Jesus's suffering and crucifixion on stage during the 2000 Oberammergau Passion Play. The play, performed daily every ten years from May through September, lasts about seven hours. The event draws over 500,000 spectators.

Karneval celebrants in elaborate costumes take a stroll during a Fasching street fair. Many Fasching enthusiasts spend all year working on and perfecting their costumes.

In 1633, the Black Plague was sweeping across Europe, wiping out entire communities. The people of this tiny Alpine village asked God to keep them safe from the deadly disease. Oberammergau was spared the fatal effects of the plague. The grateful villagers promised that in return they would present a dramatization of the passion (suffering) and death of Jesus.

The first Oberammergau Passion Play was staged in 1634 in the graveyard of the local church. In 1680, the townspeople decided to schedule the production for the first year of each new decade, a tradition that continues to this day. It is now performed on a partly open-air stage in view of the majestic Alps. Every ten years, more than 2,000 citizens of the town put on the Passion Play daily from May through September. The sixteen-act pageant depicts the sufferings of Jesus—from the Last Supper and trial to Crucifixion and Resurrection—in five and a half hours. With only a few revisions, the script is the same as that used in 1680.

Germans celebrate today in the same ways they have for centuries. They relive and commemorate important moments from their past. They drive away the hardships of everyday life with feasting. They listen to the music of the great masters. They enjoy life. To Germans, the important thing is simply that they celebrate.

# THE RELIGIONS OF GERMANY THROUGHOUT ITS HISTORY

**6**

**R**eligion has been a powerful force in Germany since the fifth century. For a thousand years Germany called its empire holy and enjoyed a special relationship with the Roman Catholic Church. Germany is also the birthplace of the Protestant movement and the center of church reform. A large part of the charm of the country's landscape comes from the steeples of its numerous churches. Many of its customs and festivals stem from religious events. Yet today religion plays only a small part in the daily life of most German citizens.

## Catholicism

The story of religion in Germany is similar to the nation's political history in that it is often changing shape. The ancient pagan beliefs of the early Germanic tribes were replaced in part by a religion brought by Roman conquerors and colonizers. That religion was a form of Christianity its critics called the Arian heresy. Heresy is a belief that is out of step with an officially accepted

belief and is usually outlawed. When the Frankish chieftain Clovis defeated the Romans, he forced all his subjects to practice Orthodox Christianity (that is, the officially accepted version of the faith).

At left, the largest mounted pilgrimage in Europe takes place every year in the town of Kötzting. About 800 riders travel from Kötzting to Steinbühl to commemorate a fifteenth-century event in which a priest rode the same route to comfort a dying man and was accompanied by townsmen for protection. Above, a pagan German priest prepares to offer a human sacrifice to the gods. Prisoners of war, serfs, and violent criminals were often sacrificed to gain the gods' favor.

This medieval manuscript illustration depicts the christening of the ancient Teutons (*left half*) and the killing of Saint Boniface (*right half*). Boniface, an Anglo-Saxon monk from Devon, England, helped convert Germany to Christianity, but was murdered by a mob of Frisian pagans.

The Orthodox Christianity of the late fifth century was Catholicism. Clovis and his successors were the champions of that faith. They, together with the popes, sent missionaries to convert the other German tribes. In the eighth century, the English monks Boniface and Willibrord also helped spread the Catholic religion throughout Germany. Boniface was so successful as a missionary that he has been called the Apostle of Germany. In addition to preaching, he destroyed items of pagan worship (such as altars and statues) and built churches and monasteries.

From the time of Clovis's conversion in 496 through the fifteenth century, Catholicism was the undisputed religion of Germany, the Holy Roman Empire. The popes crowned the elected emperors and the emperors fought against the pope's enemies. The emperors and princes gave grants of land to the bishops of the church, and many bishops became rich and powerful.

## Protestantism

A sixteenth-century German priest, Martin Luther, became troubled by the abuses he saw corrupting the church. Luther had been a monk, then a priest, then a theology

This 1539 oil-on-canvas portrait of Martin Luther was painted by German artist Lucas Cranach the Elder. Cranach painted several portraits of Luther and provided woodcut designs for the first German edition of the New Testament.

professor (a teacher of religious philosophy and doctrine). He focused on one particular abuse: the selling of indulgences. The church taught that after death everyone had to suffer some punishment for the sins he or she committed in life, even though those sins were forgiven. In an effort to raise more money among their congregations, some priests and bishops began selling "indulgences" (a sort of forgiveness). The buying of an indulgence was said to lessen the amount of punishment one would receive after death. Luther was outraged by this practice and felt it violated holy scripture.

Luther wrote down his reasons for disagreeing with the church on this matter. He composed ninety-five arguments (called theses) against indulgences. In 1517, he nailed a copy of his list to the door of All Saints Church in Wittenberg, where he taught. His purpose was to stimulate scholarly debate on the subject. The theses were written in Latin, the official language of the university and the Catholic Church. However, some-one translated the ninety-five theses into German, the language of the common people. Copies were widely distributed, widely read, and widely supported among average Germans. When church officials saw how popular Luther's ideas had become, they asked him to take his words back.

This sixteenth-century woodcut depicts Martin Luther nailing his ninety-five theses to the church door at Wittenburg in 1517.

Wartburg Castle is located on a 1230-foot (375 m) cliff overlooking the city of Eisenach. Luther lived in it while in exile following his excommunication. While there, he translated the New Testament into German.

At the Diet (meeting of leaders) in the city of Worms, Luther refused. He was excommunicated and outlawed.

Luther had not wanted to start a new religion. He simply wanted to reform the Catholic Church. That is why the movement he started is called the Protestant Reformation. It was both a protest and a reform movement but was not intended to be a schism (a formal separation from the church). People who followed Luther's ideas even after his excommunication called themselves Lutherans. When the Lutherans protested the actions and policies of the Catholic Church, they were called Protestants. Today, the term "Protestant" refers to several Christian religious groups, one of which is the Lutheran sect.

In reaction to Luther's growing protest movement, the Catholic Counter Reformation got under way. In order to address the main objection of Protestants, the Catholic Church abolished the sale of indulgences and made other reforms. In the process, they won back some of the Protestants, but the reform movements were now too powerful and established to disappear. Two separate strands of Western Christianity were now developing side by side.

The Protestant Reformation was fueled not only by religious fervor but by the desire of some to weaken the power of the Catholic Church. The princes of northern Germany, the peasants, the commercial class, and the lower clergy were eager to be free of the domination of the pope in Rome and his rich and powerful bishops. On the other hand, the emperor, the southern princes, and the higher clergy—who were benefiting from the present system—wanted to keep things as they were. This volatile mix of economics, politics, and religion resulted in the Peasants' War (1524–1526), the Thirty Years' War (1618–1648), and other bloody conflicts throughout Germany. The princes of the southern states imposed Catholicism on their subjects by force. When the wars finally ended, southern and western Germany remained Catholic while northern and central Germany were stubbornly Protestant.

## The Declining Influence of Religion in Germany

Reacting to the violent religious upheavals that had spread throughout Europe, eighteenth-century philosophers introduced a way of thinking called rationalism. Rationalism rejected the doctrines of both Catholicism and Protestantism and the emotional hysteria they provoked. Instead of a God-centered world, rationalist philosophers concentrated on natural laws and reasoning. To the rationalists, existence was not a mystery controlled by superstition or an angry God whose actions were often inexplicable. Rather, existence was very orderly, bound by certain rules and processes. Everything you needed to know about existence could be learned through observation and clear, logical thought. Saying their thinking was "enlightened" by reason rather than religion, philosophers called this period the Age of Enlightenment. The Enlightenment led many Germans away from religion.

All churches—both Catholic and Protestant—were further weakened under Adolf Hitler (1889–1995). Hitler tried to bring every aspect of Germans' daily life, including religion, under Nazi control. He appointed Nazi bishops and imposed Nazi rule on Catholic and Protestant churches alike. Many Catholics and Protestants who opposed Hitler on religious and moral grounds (some of whom hid Jews from the Nazis) became victims of Hitler's concentration camps.

After World War II (1939–1945), the influence of religion in Germany fell even further. In East Germany, the Communist government, opposed to any belief system other than Communism, severely restricted the freedom of churches and the practice of religion. Religion was removed from all public life. Religious rituals for events, such as weddings and funerals, were replaced with secular ceremonies. The church was not officially outlawed, but educational and employment opportunities were denied to citizens who professed religious faith. Forty years of official hostility to religion almost destroyed the Christian churches in East Germany. At the time of unification, more than 70 percent of East Germans said they did not believe in the existence of any god.

In West Germany, enthusiasm for religion also dropped in the decades following World War II. The shock, disgust, and guilt provoked by the Holocaust and the Nazi terror made many Germans feel like God could not possibly exist if the world was capable of such evil. As the country's economy was rebuilt and became the powerhouse of postwar Europe, many West Germans became more materialistic than spiritual. Between 1980 and 1992, more than 2 million Germans took their names off church membership rolls (which saved them from paying a church tax imposed on all members of religious institutions). Many more remained on the lists but did not attend church functions regularly or at all.

## Religion Today

Despite the fact that so many German churches are almost empty on Sundays, nearly three-fourths of Germany's population claims to belong to some religion. The majority of the population—68 percent, almost evenly divided—is Catholic or Protestant. As in the seventeenth century, Catholics reside mostly in southern and western Germany, while Protestants are clustered in the country's north and center.

Germany's Basic Law guarantees freedom of religion. Recognized churches have a privileged status as public bodies. They are supported by a tax collected from their members by the government. Religious organizations that maintain public service facilities, such as hospitals, nursing homes, schools, and day care centers, are funded by the state. Churches may provide religious education in public schools.

Like the Christian churches, Jewish institutions now have privileged status. Before World War II,

A young Jewish man attends Jewish school in Berlin. The largest Jewish communities in modern Germany are found in Frankfurt and Berlin.

Catholic nuns pray at a church in Osterhofen Altenmarkt. The influence of Catholicism in German-speaking Europe remains strong. Roughly half of all ethnic Germans are officially Roman Catholics.

approximately 600,000 Jews lived in Germany. They had lived there since ancient times and were every bit as German as non-Jewish Germans. By the end of the war, however, virtually all Jews had fled, been driven out, or were murdered. After the Nazi regime was defeated, some German Jews began returning to their homeland. With the collapse of Communism in Eastern Europe, other Jews also came to Germany from the new countries of the former Soviet Union. Today, Jews in Germany number 150,000, a number that continues to grow.

Germany also has a growing population of Muslims, totaling about 3 million. Many of them are descended from the Turkish guest workers who helped reconstruct Germany's economy after World War II. Germany's Muslim citizens are a diverse group, representing a number of different Islamic sects. Islam does not have the public structures—such as hospitals and day care—that the government requires for the religion to be granted public body status, so Islam is not taught in the state schools.

Because Germany has such a generous immigration policy that welcomes many immigrants from around the world, many religions are now being practiced there. For example, about 150,000 Buddhists and 100,000 Hindus live in Germany. This variety of religious practice and expression is a testament to Germany's postwar and post-unification commitment to tolerance.

Muslim men remove their shoes and bow toward Mecca while praying to Allah in a mosque located in the Frankfurt airport.

# THE ART AND ARCHITECTURE OF GERMANY

**7**

T he art and architecture of Germany ranges from miniature drawings in medieval manuscripts to elaborate frescoes that cover whole walls, from tiny cottages to grand castles, from plain monasteries to ornate cathedrals. Sometimes new structures were placed on top of old ones, and churches and palaces begun under one ruler were continued under others. This is why some German buildings reflect two or more architectural styles. Much German art and architecture were damaged or destroyed by Allied bombing in World War II, but many damaged examples of classical art and architecture have been restored.

## Early Art (Ninth and Tenth Centuries)

During the reign of Charlemagne, German architecture was inspired by the art of the Eastern Roman, or Byzantine, Empire. Churches were huge, symmetrical structures with a main room and wide passageways to smaller side rooms. The floor plan was generally shaped like a cross. The central chapel was often octagonal (eight-sided) with a

At left, a neighborhood of half-timbered houses rises up a hillside in Freudenberg. Half-timbered houses are common across Germany but differ in style from region to region. Above, Caspar David Friedrich (1774–1840) became the most prominent painter of the Romantic movement in Germany. Nostalgia and sentimentalism for Germany's prehistoric, primal past were a common feature of German Romanticism, as was an almost pagan feeling of awe and terror for nature. The above painting is Friedrich's *Wanderer Above the Sea and Fog* (1818).

A tenth-century manuscript illumination depicts Holy Roman Emperor Otto III seated on his throne surrounded by clerics. He reigned from 996 until his death in 1002.

domed roof made of wood. The German innovation to this model was the "westworks." The western wall of the church was raised several stories higher than the rest of the structure and bell towers stood at each end.

The Carolingian rulers (named after Charlemagne) and their successors, the Ottonians, sought to spread Christianity throughout Germany and used art to educate and impress the people. Large mosaics (a collection of small painted tiles that together form a large picture) of figures from the Bible adorned churches. Frescoes depicting biblical scenes covered their walls. Religious sculptures of ivory, bronze, and gold graced the aisles. Altars were covered in gold and cathedral doors were made of bronze.

Other than these large-scale church and building decorations, most Carolingian art was tiny in size. Miniature paintings of biblical or classical scenes were popular. Monks illustrated the manuscripts they copied with small colorful pictures called illuminations. Some of the manuscripts were enclosed in ivory covers filled with tiny carvings. Even the script, a new form called miniscule, was tiny.

## Romanesque Period (Eleventh and Twelfth Centuries)

Carolingian art forms developed gradually into the Romanesque style. The name comes from the fact that the works were patterned after the art of the ancient Roman Empire. German Romanesque churches were enormous, tall cathedrals. The domed roof was replaced with a rounded and vaulted ceiling. To support the higher roof, the vaulting was constructed of strong masonry (stone or brick) instead of wood. Heavy masonry columns further strengthened the structures. Small round

windows were placed beneath the vault. To complement the twin bell towers of the westworks, additional round or octagonal towers were added.

Most of the art of the Romanesque period was produced in the monasteries. Monks sculpted wood and bronze figures for the walls of church entryways. They shaped elaborate designs on church columns. In addition to the illuminated drawings found in manuscripts, the monks also decorated the first letter of each paragraph or chapter with creative flourishes and pictures. Most metalwork was also made for church use: candlesticks, crosses, chalices, and other items used in worship. In addition, craftsmen made jewelry and tableware of gold, silver, bronze, and enamel.

Saint Michael's Church in Hildesheim was built between 1010 and 1020. The church is famous for its wooden ceiling, painted stucco work, and bronze doors and column. This church's design typifies the Romanesque churches of the Holy Roman Empire.

## Early and High Gothic Periods (Twelfth to Fourteenth Centuries)

The name "Gothic" was given to the art and architecture of the High Middle Ages by Italian Renaissance artists years later. It was a critical term that suggested that the

This statue of a bishop holding a crucifix stands before the thirteenth-century cathedral in Limburg. Limburg is a medieval district dating back to the tenth century. It is located in the central German state Hesse.

art of the Middle Ages was as crude and barbaric as the Gothic tribes that once ravaged Europe. In reality, though, the design, techniques, and scale of the Gothic period revolutionized art.

Gothic architecture originated in France and was used primarily for cathedrals. Some Gothic castles were also built. The rounded features of Romanesque buildings became more pointed in Gothic structures. The vaulted roofs, arches, and windows reached much higher and were more narrow. Flying buttresses (external supports) were often needed to help hold up the extremely tall walls. The external supports made it possible to use lighter building materials. This, in turn, enabled large glass windows to be installed. As time went on, the windows became larger. This was done not to let in more light, but because stained-glass art had developed and become increasingly popular. The windows were mosaics of dark, richly colored glass that did not let in much light though they created dazzling, colorful effects. Despite the large size of the windows, Gothic churches were almost as dark and gloomy as the Romanesque ones.

Other than architecture, Germany's main Gothic creations were statues. In their poses and facial expressions, the sculpted figures displayed great emotion. A famous statue of this period is the Bamberg Rider, a depiction of a heroic medieval king. It was the first statue of a horse and rider to be produced in the West since the sixth century. In Gothic art, figures were idealized, often angelic or heroic, rather than realistic and flawed.

A 1498 self-portrait by German artist Albrecht Dürer at the age of twenty-seven. Albrecht Dürer was born to Hungarian parents in Nuremberg, Germany. He was the second of eighteen children.

# Renaissance, or Late Gothic, Period (Fifteenth and Sixteenth Centuries)

The word "Renaissance" means "rebirth." Renaissance art was a rebirth of the classical art forms of ancient Greece and Rome. The art, which began in Italy, explored the natural world and the human figure. In Germany, architecture was not greatly affected by the revival of classical forms. The Gothic style of building continued until the end of the sixteenth century. The visual arts, however, were greatly influenced by Renaissance styles.

The principal art form of the Renaissance was painting. Many of the paintings were religious, commissioned by bishops and nobles for their churches. Panel painting was very popular during this time. Various related scenes would be painted on several large panels of wood, which would then be joined together to form one grand work. The panels were placed behind altars or used to separate areas of the churches. The works were narrative pictures, meaning they told a story and usually involved several main figures and a crowd of people in the background.

Portrait painting first became popular in the Renaissance. Great attention was given to every

Albrecht Dürer's *Lamentation Over the Dead Christ* depicts the sorrow of Jesus's mother, Mary Magdalene, and the apostle John, among others, after they have brought Jesus down from the cross.

detail of the picture. People looked very realistic, even down to the pores of their skin and complicated folds of their clothing. Two of the best-known German portrait painters were Hans Holbein the Younger (circa 1497–1543) and Lucas Cranach the Elder (1472–1553). These two men also made woodcuts and engravings for book illustrations.

The person who did the most to bring the artistic styles of the Italian Renaissance to Germany was a master of every form of art. He did landscapes, panels, portraits, woodcuts, and engravings. Albrecht Dürer defined the Renaissance in Germany. He was so important that Germans call the period *Dürerzeit* (Age of Dürer). He produced at least 70 paintings, 350 woodcuts, 900 drawings, and a number of essays on art. His works influenced artists throughout Europe.

## Baroque and Rococo Periods (Seventeenth and Eighteenth Centuries)

Following the Renaissance, art became more elaborate and complex. More decorations, more flourishes, more gold, more of everything was what characterized the baroque period. The many princes vying for power in Germany tried to show their wealth and influence by building castles that were more magnificent than those of their neighbors. Baroque buildings had massive portals (entryways), broad staircases, and dozens of rooms.

The artistic ideal of the baroque—and its even more extravagant extension, rococo—was *Gesamtkunstwerk*: the blending of all the arts. This ideal was accomplished in the grand castles. Paintings, sculptures, and frescoes were all part of the castles' architectural designs. Germany had baroque artists, but most of the grand palaces and churches of the period were the works of designers imported from France and Italy.

## Modern Periods

In the late eighteenth century, art took a 180-degree turn. Rococo curves and curlicues were replaced by the straight lines of neoclassicism. In a return to ancient Greek design, plain columns and simple domes were the primary design features.

At left, the Wies Church that stands on the slopes of the Ammergau Alps was built in 1746 by Dominikus Zimmermann. It was to be a pilgrimage church *in der Wies* (in the meadows). The church's dome, seen here, was painted by Dominikus's brother, Johann Baptist. It depicts a scene from the day of judgment in which the door to paradise has been closed and the throne of judgment vacated.

Paintings no longer used biblical subjects, but turned instead to figures from ancient Greek and Roman mythology. For example, the Brandenburg Gate, a triumphal arch built in Berlin from 1788 to 1791 for King Frederick Wilhelm II, resembles the Greek Acropolis.

In reaction to the simplicity, clarity, and coldness of neo-classicism, the nineteenth century began by embracing Romantic art. Art of this period was characterized by an almost medieval sense of mystery and gloom. This period is sometimes called revivalism because it revived Germany's earlier, pre-Renaissance styles. New castles and churches were built in the Romanesque or Gothic style, while older structures received neo-Gothic additions. In addition, painters again returned to religious subjects.

By the late nineteenth century, art had become less oriented toward the courts and the churches. Instead, it began to embrace the common people and ordinary

Max Ernst (1891–1976) was a twentieth-century German painter who helped found surrealism, an art movement devoted to dreamlike images that explored the human subconscious. This painting, *Bryce Canyon Translation*, was inspired by the eerily beautiful rock formations of southern Utah.

materials. Artists painted pictures of common folk doing ordinary things, like working or playing. Building designers began using everyday steel, concrete, and glass and focusing on the function of the structure rather than its appearance. They stripped their designs of frills and fancy fronts. Walter Gropius (1883–1969) founded the Bauhaus school that sought to marry art and practicality in architecture, painting, sculpture, furniture making, and other crafts. The school's International Style was adopted all over the world.

For many years after World War II, Germany's architects devoted themselves to rebuilding the bombed and broken country. Construction had to be quick and inexpensive because people needed homes and companies needed offices as quickly as possible. Given these conditions, little thought could be given to art. Now, however, much attention is being placed on restoring some of the nation's historic and cultural landmarks. And today's artists are looking for ways to express the spirit of a unified Germany.

# THE LITERATURE AND MUSIC OF GERMANY

8

In the earliest days of the Germanic tribes, literature and music were one and the same. The ancient stories were sung, not read from a manuscript or book. The German peoples had not yet created a written form of their spoken language. So the *lied* or *lay* (song) kept the history and legends of the people alive. Under Charlemagne, monks began writing down some of these legends and songs, and music and literature began to develop along separate paths.

## The Middle Ages (Ninth to Fourteenth Centuries)

The earliest written work in the German language is the *Hildebrandslied* (Song of Hildebrand) from the *Dietrich* saga. It was committed to writing around 800. Many of the early copies of this and other pagan legends were later burned by fanatical churchmen. A part of the *Hildebrandslied* survived, however, because its pages were reused as a cover for a religious book.

In keeping with Charlemagne's policy of forced conversions of pagans to Christianity, the monks "Christianized" the old pagan stories. People also wrote religious ballads that used the same form

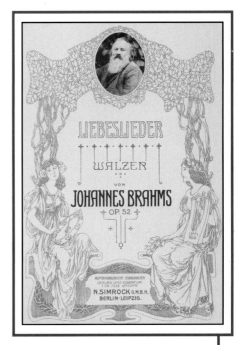

At left is a 1764 portrait of German composer Johann Sebastian Bach. Bach began composing at the age of nine. Unlike many leading composers of his time, Bach never left his home country, even for a holiday. His entire life and career were spent in Germany. Before Johannes Brahms became a composer, he was a pianist. As a composer, he had a particular fondness for piano pieces. Above is an original cover page for Brahms's *Liebeslieder Walzer*, a waltz for four hands (two pianists playing one piano simultaneously).

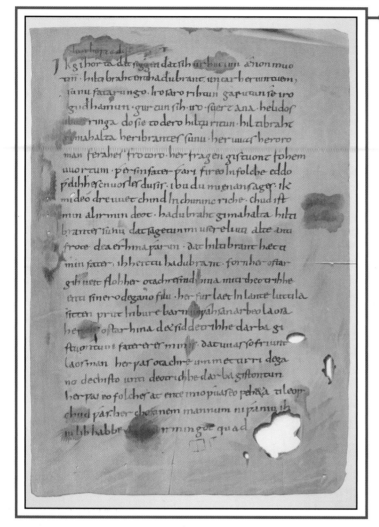

This is one of the pages from the only preserved manuscript copy of the *Hildebrandslied*. It dates back to around AD 850. The *Hildebrandslied* is an epic tale set during the fifth century and is part of the *Dietrich* saga.

as older heroic poems. *Heliand* (Savior), a Saxon epic of the life of Christ, was probably written to help the newly converted Saxons learn the basics of the Christian faith. It tells the Jesus story as if it were a medieval romance, with Christ cast as a warring knight.

During the early Middle Ages, most of the literature was religious. In the High Middle Ages (1100–1400), however, some secular stories also appeared. Some of these were old legends that had finally been written down, such as the *Nibelungenlied*. Others were new tales of adventure, like the ballad of Parsifal. This ballad is one of many medieval European stories concerned with the search for the holy grail, the wine cup or bowl Jesus used at the Last Supper. Some court epics were love stories, such as Gottfried von Strassburg's tragic account of *Tristan und Isolde*. Others featured animals instead of people, like Heinrich von Glîchezaere's *Reynard the Fox*. The stories were sung by *Spielleute*, or wandering minstrels, who traveled from castle to castle.

In addition to epics, lyric poetry flourished in the medieval courts. *Minnesingers* (literally, "singers of love songs") wrote love songs and religious tunes. They were usually lesser nobles, and they performed in the castles of higher nobility. They

accompanied themselves with harps, fiddles, lutes, or other stringed instruments. The most famous minnesingers were Walther von der Vogelweide and Wolfram von Eschenbach.

## Renaissance (Fourteenth to Sixteenth Centuries)

Toward the end of the thirteenth century, medieval society began to change. Peasants asserted themselves and a middle class developed. Simple folk songs of the common people, *Volkslieder*, became popular. Some musical craftsmen began to earn a living by writing and performing music. They set up schools and formed guilds (associations of people with similar interests, trades, or jobs). A poet/songwriter would begin as an apprentice (a student to a master), rise to the level of journeyman (someone who works for another person), and finally become a *Meistersinger*—a respected and sought-after master of his art. These middle-class Meistersingers eventually replaced the aristocratic minnesingers.

The Protestant Reformation that shook Germany also strongly affected its literature and music. Martin Luther's translation of the Latin

In this thirteenth-century manuscript illumination, a ruler judges a singing contest between famous minnesingers.

Bible into the language of the people opened up the world of literature to the average person, rather than just monks and nobles. As a result, the romantic epic poems and love songs associated with the royal court began to yield to poems, plays, and stories that used comedy and satire that would appeal to average people. In addition to the carefully crafted songs of the Meistersingers, music of this time also included religious hymns. Luther translated the Latin church songs into German and wrote several of his own, usually set to the tunes of the Volkslieder.

## Baroque Period (Seventeenth to Eighteenth Centuries)

Very little writing and musical composition was produced during the Thirty Years' War that followed the Protestant Reformation. When artistic creation picked up again, most of it reflected the despair felt by Germans following the long and bloody war. For example, Andreas Gryphius's poem "Tears of the Fatherland" described the horrors of the conflict. In Hans Jacob Christoff von Grimmelshausen's *The Adventures of a Simpleton*, the first German novel, the hero becomes a hermit after the war to escape society's violence and hatred.

Baroque music, like baroque architecture, was complex and ornate. Earlier music had been mainly sung, often with plain melodies and little musical accompaniment. Now choral music was becoming more complex, with many voices singing in multipart harmony. Non-choral instrumental music also began to grow in popularity. The two

This handwritten score is part of a piece Johann Sebastian Bach wrote for and presented to his wife. Bach's second wife, Anna Magdalena, was a soprano. Many of their children became musicians or composers.

most famous musicians of this period were Johann Sebastian Bach (1685–1750) and Georg Friedrich Handel (1685–1759), both of whom composed choral and instrumental works that are still considered among the highest achievements of classical music.

## Classical Period (Late Eighteenth to Early Nineteenth Centuries)

The play *Sturm und Drang* (Storm and Stress) by Friedrich Maximilian von Klinger gave its name to the brief period in literature (1767–1785) that ushered in the classical era. Works of this period featured heroes struggling against their natures or fates in an attempt to become superior beings. The great names of this movement and of German classical literature were Johann Wolfgang von Goethe (1749–1832) and Friedrich von Schiller (1759–1805). Classical literature was influenced by the ideas of the Prussian-born philosopher Immanuel Kant (1724–1804) who discussed the supreme importance and

This 1756 portrait depicts composer Georg Friederich Handel. During his career, Handel composed over fifty operas, twenty-three oratorios (religious choral works), and several instrumental pieces. Among his most famous works are *Messiah* (which includes the "Hallelujah Chorus") and *Water Music*.

A nineteenth-century illustration depicts Faust and Mephistopheles (a devil) in the witches' hut. The story of Faust—who sells his soul in order to gain forbidden knowledge—has been the inspiration for numerous plays, compositions, novels, and poems.

worth of human consciousness and reason in the pursuit of knowledge. Influenced by these ideas and looking back to their German folk culture, poets and playwrights wrote of common heroes struggling intensely against their own limits and those of the external world to reach for the ideal of greatness. The struggle often ends in defeat or tragedy. In Goethe's *Faust*, for example, the main character makes a pact with the devil in order to gain greater knowledge and power.

In classical music, new forms were developed that made greater use of instruments: concertos, sonatas, string quartets, and symphonies. The Austrian capital, Vienna, became the world's center for classical music, as the Viennese composers Wolfgang Amadeus Mozart and Franz Joseph Haydn composed masterpiece after masterpiece. The two best-known German classical musicians of this period also studied and worked in Vienna: Ludwig van Beethoven (1770–1827) and Christoph Willibald Gluck (1714–1787). Beethoven

This is an 1819 portrait of composer Ludwig van Beethoven by German artist Karl Stieler. In his early thirties, Beethoven realized he was going deaf. He often became very angry and depressed, which many critics think accounts for his moody, stormy music.

This 1880 page from Richard Wagner's opera *Nibelungenlied* is part of Siegfried's death scene. The *Nibelungenlied* consists of four operas: *Das Rheingold, Die Walkurie* (The Valkyrie), *Siegfried*, and *Gotterdammerung* (Twilight of the Gods). Wagner (*seen below*) considered himself the "most German of men" and the embodiment of the German spirit.

composed a huge variety of orchestral works and Gluck wrote operas.

## Romantic Period (Nineteenth Century)

The political revolutions that began in the United States and France just before the nineteenth century inspired a feeling across Europe that the common people and the individual were as important as any king, priest, or nobleman. This sentiment swept through Germany and led to an increased interest in examining the struggles and stories of the common man and woman and the old tales of German folk heroes. The emotional exuberance of the revolutionary spirit also found its way into music and literature. Artists rejected the rationalism of previous generations and described people and nature in more sentimental terms. They turned to old stories and national heroes for inspiration. The Grimm brothers collected their folktales. Musicians Carl Maria von Weber (1786–1826) and Richard Wagner (1813–1883) wrote romanticized versions of German myths and legends. In his magnificent operas, Wagner immortalized the

The philosopher and economist Karl Marx appears at left in this 1875 photograph. Below is a page from an original, handwritten draft of his *Communist Manifesto*.

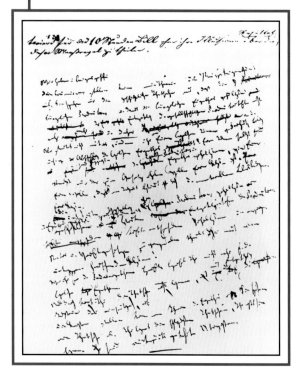

stories of the Niebelungs, Parsifal, Lohengrin, and Tristan and Isolde.

Although the opera, with its spectacular staging and emotional music, was the grandest expression of Romantic themes, other forms also emerged. Johannes Brahms, Robert Schumann, and the Austrian Franz Schubert perfected the *Lied*, or art song. Using less instrumentation, these men composed melodies for the Romantic poetry of their day. Felix Mendelssohn and Richard Strauss wrote program music—short orchestral pieces that used music to depict stories or scenes. Mendelssohn's "Wedding March" is still played at many weddings today.

Romanticism faded into Realism when the ideals of the revolutions that were sweeping Europe failed to effect any concrete changes in Germany. In addition, Napoléon—who had risen to power at the head of a newly democratic France—had become a power-hungry dictator bent on taking over all of Europe, including Germany. The Romantic dream of democratic revolution began to feel like a nightmare. Novels, the main literary form at this time, were political statements, harshly criticizing the country's leaders and German society.

Working in the midst of this turmoil, Germany's late-nineteenth-century philosophers influenced the world for decades to come. Friedrich Engels (1820–1895) and

Karl Marx (1818–1883) developed ideas that became the basis for Socialism and Communism. The philosopher Friedrich Wilhelm Nietzsche (1844–1900) promoted the concept of the *Übermensch* (a superman, someone beyond the law and moral codes of average humans), from which Hitler took the notion of a superior race.

## Twentieth Century

The twentieth century, a very difficult time for Germany, cannot be defined by a single literary or musical style. Music ranged from classical to pop, from orchestral pieces for operas to simple tunes for films.

Literature was also quite varied. It included novels, short stories, poetry, and plays. Most of it was colored by discouragement following Germany's defeat in World War I, dissatisfaction with Nazi policies preceding World War II, and grief over social conditions following Germany's second military defeat. Thomas Mann's (1875–1955) novels were critiques of German society. Hermann Hesse

Actors on stage present a scene from Bertolt Brecht's play *The Caucasian Chalk Circle*, a highly political play about a dispute over land and a parallel struggle for custody of a child. Brecht was a Communist and fled the Nazi regime. He lived in exile in the United States, where he wrote this play and many of his other most famous works. He eventually left for Switzerland due to anti-Communist sentiments in the United States.

Nobel Prize-winner Günter Grass (1927–), seen in this 1981 photograph, is best known in the United States for his novel *The Tin Drum*, about a Nazi-era boy who refuses to grow up and is eventually committed to a psychiatric hospital. Before becoming a writer, Grass was a coal miner and received a trade education in stone masonry.

(1877–1962) wrote of the search for new values and identity after the disillusionment of war. Both were Nobel Prize winners. Rainer Maria Rilke (1875–1926) wrote love poems and religious verse. In the 1920s, Bertolt Brecht pioneered the "epic theater"—a dramatic account of a historic event enhanced with music, masks, dialogue, and commentary. Epic theater pieces were read or sung in the cabarets (nightclub-like cafés) of the cities. Because some of the works criticized the Nazi regime and some were written by Jews, many of the books and song sheets of this period were burned in huge public bonfires. A number of the writers and some of the musicians were exiled or imprisoned by Hitler. He preferred the works of Wagner, who celebrated the glories of German history.

After Hitler's defeat, some of Germany's outlawed artists returned to West Germany. They created a new form of literature: the radio play. In these plays, the authors grappled with the problems of postwar devastation, poverty, and guilt over the horrors of Nazism. Some questioned whether Germany could ever produce works of beauty again. The Nobel Prize winners Günter Grass and Heinrich Böll (1917–1985), as well as several other writers and musicians, proved that Germany still possessed a creative spirit and a humane soul.

## Modern Literature and Music

Germany, a nation of frequently shifting borders and a changing population, has long had difficulty defining itself. Since reunification in 1990, formerly East German and West German writers have tried to understand what it means to be

German at the dawn of the twenty-first century. Their novels, poetry, and dramas have received international recognition.

The music for which Germany is so famous can still be heard in many theaters, concert halls, and festivals throughout the country. Artists are continuing to produce new music in older forms long cherished by Germans: operas, musical theater, cabaret music, and jazz. German youth, however, tend to embrace the modern popular musical forms first created in other Western nations: rock, heavy metal, punk, and rap. Berlin's annual Love Parade draws a million young people to a celebration of Germany's latest and ongoing contributions to modern music.

German musicians, led by the group Kraftwerk whose album appears here, introduced the world to a new form of electronic popular music in the 1970s. Relying heavily on synthesizers and impersonal, mechanical lyrics, Kraftwerk had an enormous influence on artists like David Bowie and Devo and inspired the development of electronica in the 1990s.

# FAMOUS FOODS AND RECIPES OF GERMANY

## 9

T he German equivalent of "Enjoy your meal" is *Guten Appetit or* "Good appetite." Guten Appetit also expresses what many Germans have—a hearty appetite. Some still follow the time-honored custom of eating five meals a day. About two hours after the first meal of the day comes the second breakfast, usually pastries with coffee. Lunch is the main meal of the day. Between lunch and dinner Germans eat a late afternoon snack of sausage and cheeses. The final meal is traditionally a supper of cold meats and bread with cheese, pickles, and possibly a salad or fruit.

## Meats and Fish

Meat is a very large part of the average German diet. German farmers raise beef and dairy cows, pigs, and sheep. Because pigs are so plentiful, far outnumbering other livestock, pork is the primary meat of the German diet. Because they eat so much meat, Germans have had to devise ways of preserving and storing it. They smoke, salt, and

marinate it, creating what is the unofficial national dish: *Wurst*, or sausage. Germany has more than 1,500 different kinds of sausages. They are made of ground pork *(Mettwurst)*, liver *(Leberwurst)*, veal *(Weisswurst)*, mixed meats *(Fleischwurst)*, or meat and blood *(Blutwurst)*. Some are eaten raw, while others are boiled, roasted, smoked, or fried. Nearly every town has its own distinctive sausage specialty.

At left is a delicious, cherry-topped Black Forest cake. Black Forest cake is usually decorated with chocolate shavings or sprinkles. The cake is named after the Black Forest of Bavaria, where the recipe is said to have originated. Above, a vendor in Munich sells piping-hot pretzels of all sizes. Pretzels were invented by a seventh-century monk who found a use for extra bread dough. The pretzel shape is thought to evoke the crossing of arms in prayer. Hard pretzels are thought to have been invented in Pennsylvania when a baker left a batch in the oven for too long.

This plate of roast pork and dumplings forms a traditional, hearty German dinner. Thick, tasty gravy is an essential part of the meal. Dumplings are typically soaked in gravy before they are eaten.

Pork is also served as roasts, chops, and pig knuckles. Some is made into ham. In the Black Forest, hams are smoked over fires made from fir cones and covered with beef blood to give them a black coating. Beef is fixed in many ways, such as roasts, steaks, and stews. Beef is also ground and formed into meatloaves and meatballs. Tougher cuts of meat may be roasted in wine or vinegar (*Sauerbraten*). Tender pieces of veal are frequently breaded and pan cooked (*Wienerschnitzel*). Meat is also often served in gravy on open-faced sandwiches, and eaten with knife and fork.

Hunters may feast on roast venison (from deer), rabbit, and game birds. Germany's seas, lakes, and rivers yield a rich variety of fish. The seas in the north are known for their herring. The rivers teem with pike, sole, and turbot. Salmon can be found in the Rhine. People near the mountain lakes and Alpine streams eat trout. Lake Constance alone has thirty-five different kinds of fish. Carp is a prized fish in Germany, and smoked eels are commonly served as appetizers or snacks.

Meat and fish dishes are often accompanied by some kind of starch or vegetable. With their meat and fish, Germans eat potatoes, bread, or potato dumplings, and a chewy noodle called *Spätzle*. Cabbage is common and is often pickled, producing sauerkraut. Nearly every German meal includes bread.

## Breads and Cheeses

Germans make 200 different types of bread, 30 different kinds of rolls, and 1,200 varieties of pastries. Bread is such a staple in Germany that the second breakfast is called *Brotzeit* (bread time) and the nighttime meal is *Abendbrot* (evening bread). Made from wheat, rye, and pumpernickel, German breads are often very dark and heavy.

Germany's large dairy farms supply lots of butter and cheese for the breads. Germany produces several cheeses that originated in other countries: Camembert, Brie,

German breads are usually thick, dark, highly textured, and very flavorful and filling. Rye flour is often used.

Parmesan, Swiss, and Limberger. But some cheeses are distinctly German inventions. Bruder Basil, originally made by monks in Bavaria, is smoked over beech wood. Tilsit was accidentally created by Dutch immigrants who were trying to make their native Gouda. Other uniquely German cheeses are Montagnolo, Regina Blu, and melt-in-your-mouth Butterkäse.

## Sweets

The ample supply of butter and cream allows Germans to concoct some wonderful pastries. The country is famous for its apple strudel, which is especially good with Bavarian cream. German cookbooks are filled with recipes for delicate cookies, rich tortes, and delicious cakes. One specialty is *Schwarzwälder Torte*—Black Forest cake. It is made of chocolate layers filled with cherries and whipped cream.

## Foreign Fare

Because of Germany's location at the center of Europe, German food has been influenced by the cuisine of neighboring countries. Many restaurants and some homes cook in the French, Italian, Hungarian, Russian, Swedish, or Greek styles. As

Heart-shaped gingerbread cookies are decorated with romantic messages, such as *Ich Liebe Dich* (I love you).

# Pfeffernüsse
## (Pepper nut cookies)

These are traditional German Christmas cookies, originally meant to be dunked in wine during Christmas parties and holiday visiting.

### Ingredients
¼ C. light molasses
¼ C. butter
2 eggs, beaten
4 C. sifted flour
¼ C. honey
1 tsp. baking soda
1 tsp. cinnamon
¼ tsp. cloves
½ tsp. nutmeg
Dash of pepper and salt

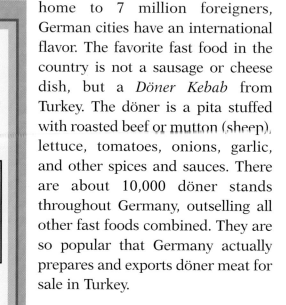

### Preparation
Combine molasses and butter in saucepan; cook and stir until butter melts. Cool to room temperature. Stir in eggs.
Sift together remaining ingredients, mixing well. Chill several hours or overnight.
Shape chilled dough into 1-inch balls. Bake on greased cookie sheet at 375°F for 12 minutes.
Cool. Roll in powdered sugar.

Makes about 5 dozen cookies.

home to 7 million foreigners, German cities have an international flavor. The favorite fast food in the country is not a sausage or cheese dish, but a *Döner Kebab* from Turkey. The döner is a pita stuffed with roasted beef or mutton (sheep), lettuce, tomatoes, onions, garlic, and other spices and sauces. There are about 10,000 döner stands throughout Germany, outselling all other fast foods combined. They are so popular that Germany actually prepares and exports döner meat for sale in Turkey.

## Beverages

All this hearty food is generally washed down with beer or wine. German wines, famed and enjoyed throughout the world, are not native to Germany. Romans brought their grapes with them as they sought to colonize the land beyond the northern boundaries of their empire. The vineyards they planted spread throughout the valleys of the Rhine and its tributaries. The cool climate of the Rhineland produces some of the world's finest white wines. Only a few vineyards grow grapes for red wines.

Germans drink less wine per capita (per person) than their European neighbors, but more beer per person than in any country (with Belgium a close second). Nearly every city has at least one brewery. Germany produces hundreds of different kinds of beers and, as with German food, each region has its own specialty. Most German beers

At a popular beer hall in Munich, Bavarians spend time with friends.

have an alcohol content below 5 percent. Beer is considered healthy and those that contain less than 1 percent alcohol are served to children. Germans actually drink more milk than wine, but more beer than milk. Beer is Germany's second-most popular drink. The beverage that Germans consume more than any other is coffee.

## Restaurants

Germany has a number of different types of eateries in addition to the traditional restaurant *(Gasthäus* or *Gasthof)*. The second breakfast is often taken in a *Konditorei* (pastry shop) or café. The afternoon meal may be eaten in a *Ratskeller*, located in the cellar of a historic town hall, or grabbed at a *Schnellgaststätte* (fast food restaurant). Food is plentiful in any wine parlor *(Weinstube)*, beer cellar *(Bierkeller)*, pub *(Beirstube* or *Kneipe)*, or beer garden *(Biergarten)*.

In these restaurants, patrons usually seat themselves. When the only available seats are at tables that are already occupied, taking these seats is not only acceptable but expected. Meeting new people in this way is one of the attractions of the popular beer gardens. Another custom that may surprise non-Germans is the presence of dogs in restaurants. Germans love their pets and sometimes bring them along to meals. Restaurant staff often provides bowls of water for the patrons' dogs.

A sign hanging outside a Heidelberg restaurant invites diners in.

# DAILY LIFE AND CUSTOMS IN GERMANY

## 10

**G**ermany is a little smaller than the state of Montana, but it has more people than the ten largest U.S. states combined. It is the third-most densely populated nation of Europe, with 600 people per square mile (about 230 people per sq km). In the industrial regions of the Rhine and Ruhr valleys, population density is about 2,800 per square mile (1,100 per sq km). Most Germans live in small towns and villages; only one-third of the population lives in large cities. In urban areas people live very close together.

Germans make up for these crowded conditions by creating a sense of privacy around their homes. They often fence in their front- and backyards and keep their doors closed. Even though their homes look inviting, with bright flowers in sunny window boxes, many Germans are so private and reserved that they do not easily welcome guests.

## Shopping

The stereotype of the German passion for order and cleanliness is evident in any of the nation's shopping areas. Germany does not have many supermarkets because its citizens prefer tidy rows of little shops that

At left, a craftsman builds a hand-carved and -painted cuckoo clock. Cuckoo clocks originated in the Black Forest. During the long winter months there, the farms were snowed-in and the people spent their time building cuckoo clocks of many styles with rich and varied carvings. When summer finally arrived, the clocks were sold by peddlers throughout Europe. Above: In order to air them out, pillows are placed in the window of a medieval-era half-timbered house in Bad Wimpfen.

specialize in certain products, such as a butcher, a greengrocer, a fruit shop, a bakery, etc. Every morning, the steps of each of these stores are swept clean. By law, no shop may open before 6 AM, and they must close precisely at 8 PM on weekdays and Saturdays. They may not open at all on Sundays. In many large cities, stores are now allowed to stay open until 9 PM once a week.

A centuries-old German custom is the open-air market. Market days are held once or twice a week throughout the year in small villages and big cities. Like the shops, each stand at the market has one kind of product: fruits and vegetables, eggs, clothes, books, or household utensils. The sticker prices are firm; Germans do not like to haggle and bargain. Many people prefer the more festive atmosphere and lower prices of the markets. They are, of course, kept as clean and orderly as the shops.

## Animals

Germans love animals, especially their dogs. They take their pets with them to the banks, cafés, beauty shops, and wherever else they have business to conduct. Germans are so fond of their pets that animals are protected under the nation's constitution. Germans have built grassy bridges over their highways to allow animals to

cross safely without danger of being struck by a car. There are steel tunnels running beneath the same roadways to allow amphibians, such as frogs and salamanders, to cross under the road in similar safety.

In German, *Autobahn* means "high-speed road." The Autobahn was built in the 1930s and today has a total length of about 7,500 miles (11,980 km). While there is no enforced speed limit for passenger cars, there are speed limits for large trucks, trailers, and buses. The "suggested" speed for cars is 80 mph (130 km/hr).

## Transportation

German wildlife needs all the help it can get crossing the roads because German drivers love to speed! Germany is the only European country with no speed limit posted on its famed highways, the Autobahn. They have a recommended limit of about 80 miles per hour (130 km/h), but cars can go as fast as they dare.

Cars are only one method of transportation in Germany. The best way of getting from one city to another is by train. Within the large cities, the easiest way of getting around is by bus, streetcar, or subway. Cities on major waterways also use ferries. A common method of transportation throughout the country is bicycling. It is very common to see little children, elderly men and women, and everyone in

between riding bicycles to get where they're going or simply for pleasure.

## Recreation

Bicycle lanes line many of Germany's roads. Bicycle paths skirt some of the country's rivers and connect some of its most scenic towns. Enthusiasts can ride mountain bikes in Bavaria or pedal along the flat land of the northern coast. They can take a train to wherever they wish to begin riding and rent a bike at the train station. Germans love cycling because they are very active people and enjoy being outdoors. They also enjoy weekend walks in the countryside or forests and strolls through the many city parks.

A favorite outdoor recreation is hiking, especially in the mountains. Southern Germany is laced with 9,300 miles (15,000 km) of Alpine hiking trails. Camping and skiing are also popular activities. Some ski downhill in the Alps of Bavaria and others go cross-country skiing in the lower mountains of the Black Forest.

A team of young soccer players gather for a group shot after a game. Soccer is said to be Germany's most beloved, most watched, and most played sport. Many Germans consider soccer to be the national sport. German teams have won several World Cups and many European championships.

The most popular German sport is soccer (known in Europe as football). Germany embraced the game in the early twentieth century, along with the rest of Europe. Soccer was only fifty years old when Germans started playing the game, and their teams quickly rose to become world champions. Nearly three-quarters of the population watches international soccer matches on television even when Germany is not competing. The country has children's, youth, adult, and professional soccer clubs.

Many other sports have large followings. One in three citizens belongs to some specialized sport club—gymnastics, rifle, track and field, tennis, swimming, handball, or table

Ski slopes dot the hills in Feldberg, where the highest peak in the Black Forest is found. In addition to its popular ski resort, Feldberg also features a health resort and nature reserve.

Berlin has long been home to a vibrant nightlife. It is best known for its cabarets, in which performers mix song, dance, poetry, music, comedy, and drama. The Chameleon Cabaret in Berlin usually features a band, acrobats, stand-up comics, and singers. It is located in Hackesche Höfe, a gigantic shopping and entertainment complex.

tennis. Tennis jumped in popularity in 1985, when Boris Becker became the first German to win the men's singles at Wimbledon. A common recreational game in Germany is *Kegeln*—nine-pin bowling. It is much like American bowling without the headpin and with smaller, hole-less balls. There are Kegel clubs, but millions of people play the game without benefit of organized leagues.

When the very active Germans want to rest, they play *Skat*, a card game for three people. As with other German games and pastimes, people who enjoy Skat organize themselves into clubs and have regular tournaments.

## Entertainment

Entertainment in Germany ranges from lively beer festivals to serious operas. The nation's long tradition of music and drama has given today's Germans hundreds of theaters, opera houses, and concert halls to choose from and attend. Some of the theaters showcase the classical music and plays of Germany's past. Others feature

Marlene Dietrich was a famous cabaret singer and actress in Germany in the 1930s. She became a U.S. citizen in the 1940s and pursued a Hollywood film career. Dietrich appeared in over fifty films spanning seven decades and performed in Las Vegas and on Broadway. She spent the last thirteen years of her life in Paris and died there in 1992.

new performers and foreign entertainers. People can choose from symphonies, films, musicals, operettas, ballet, and jazz. If they prefer not to sit and passively enjoy culture, they can wander through a museum in almost any city or town. Or they can dance at one of the many nightclubs in the larger cities.

For really lively entertainment, there is bound to be a festival under way somewhere in Germany at any given moment. These are especially inviting because most are held outdoors. There is a huge variety from which to choose: an international toy festival in Nürnberg, a sailing race in Kiel in Schleswig-Holstein, Pied Piper plays in Hameln, one of the world's largest car shows in Frankfurt, a medieval festival in Rothenburg-ob-der-Tauber, and the spectacular fireworks of the Rhine in Flames river festivals. At nearly any time and at any place, there is something fun to do in Germany!

This is a still photograph from the enormously popular 1998 German film *Lola Rennt* (*Run Lola Run*), starring internationally popular actors Franka Potente (pictured) and Moritz Bleibtreu and directed by Tom Tykwer.

# EDUCATION AND WORK IN GERMANY

**11**

G ermany has always been a world leader in the field of education. During the early Middle Ages—which some historians call the Dark Ages because of the reduction in learning and art following the fall of the Roman Empire— German monks kept literature and culture alive for all of Europe by copying classic texts that would have otherwise been lost or destroyed during the barbarian invasions. Germans founded some of the world's first universities. A university was established

in Prague (now the capital of the Czech Republic, then part of the Holy Roman Empire) in 1348, in Heidelberg in 1386, and in other German cities soon thereafter. Medieval schools taught religion as well as the language and learning of ancient Rome. They were only open to clergy, nobility, and some government officials, however.

During the Protestant Reformation, Martin Luther called for the government to provide schooling for all Germans, rich and poor. Some of the Protestant states set up primary schools (the equivalent of North America's elementary schools) for children. Luther's disciple, Melanchthon, began secondary schools (the North American equivalent of high schools). Following the Protestant lead, the Catholic states also established schools for those who could afford them.

At left, a high-tech Mercedes-Benz showroom is both a proud symbol of Germany's industrial and engineering might and a shining example of the innovative architectural energy characteristic of post-unification Berlin. Above, a multi-colored Volkswagen Beetle brightens the streets of Munich. Ferdinand Porsche (the founder of the Porsche motor company) designed the first Volkswagen.

Two young school children are tutored in English by their *Grundschule* (elementary school) teacher. By the time a child has finished Grundschule, he or she should be able to read, speak, and write English. Children between the ages of six and ten attend Grundschule.

Until the twentieth century, Germany had two separate school systems: the most wealthy 10 percent of the school-age population went to *Gymnasium* (secondary school), and everyone else stopped their education at the end of primary school. After the end of the Nazi era, during which Hitler turned the schools into centers for teaching Nazi doctrine to Germany's youth, the entire system was completely revamped. As a result, Germany's educational system is once again a model for other Western nations to follow.

## Primary Education

Germany was one of the first nations to formally educate all of its young children. In 1837, Friedrich Froebel opened a school for three- to seven-year-olds. He called it *Kindergarten*, which means "children's garden." Kindergarten is not part of the German public school system, so children do not have to attend. However, two-thirds of those between the ages of three and six do go to kindergarten.

Children at a Gymnasium study with the help of laptop computers. At the age of eleven, German students leave Grundschule for either a Hauptschule (main school), Realschule (technical or business), or Gymnasium (academic). Gymnasium graduates usually go on to university.

After kindergarten, school is free and children must attend for twelve years. Each Land regulates its own schools. There are many small differences from one Land to another, but the basic educational system is the same nationwide. From age six, children attend *Grundschule* (basic school) for four to six years. Parents make the first day of school fun for their children by sending them off with large colorful cones filled with candy and toys.

## Secondary Schools

After Grundschule, children are channeled into one of three programs based on their test scores. The top 25 percent of students go to a Gymnasium, which prepares them for a university. Another 25 percent is placed in a *Realschule* (practical school). These vocational schools train students for office jobs and professions such as nursing and government service. The lowest-performing group of students—about half the total—attends *Hauptschule* (main school). Here students receive a general education before beginning apprenticeships. From the Hauptschule, they either enter the workforce or go on to a vocational college. In a few Länder, the three programs are all available within one school called the *Gesamtschule* (comprehensive school).

The German education system is quite strict. Once placed on a certain track, students can seldom change to a different program. The course of study is also strict, concentrating on traditional academic subjects. Every student, regardless of his or her program, is required to take English. Gymnasium students must study a foreign

language. Pop quizzes and oral tests are frequently given. The Gymnasium offers few, if any, elective classes. Instead, most courses are required and not chosen by the student based on his or her personal interest. German schools do not generally have after-school sports, clubs, or other activities. They do not even have lunch. The school day generally lasts only from 8 AM to 1 PM. After classes, children are expected to spend two or three hours on homework.

## Universities and Vocational Schools

At age nineteen, Gymnasium students take a test to determine if they will get into a university. The test is very difficult, lasting up to six hours per subject. Those who pass are able to attend some of the most prestigious institutions in Europe. Although Germany has nearly 300 universities, that number is not enough to accommodate all the students who want to attend. For this reason, students cannot choose the school they want, but they must accept the one assigned to them. The cost to the student to attend university is very small because the universities are funded by the Länder and the central government.

For those not attending university, Germany has the best vocational training program in all of Europe. Almost half the population age fifteen to nineteen enrolls in *Berufsschule* (vocational school) for two or three years. Students spend about two days a week in the classroom, gaining formal education in one of about 400 job specialties. They spend the other three days as apprentices, receiving a small wage and on-the-job training. The company the apprentice works for pays his or her wages, and the Land pays for the classroom training. After apprenticeship, students can continue their education at one of the many technical or nursing colleges throughout the country.

## Work

The vocational education program produces highly skilled, specialized workers. And since many of the apprentices are hired by the company that trained them, they become loyal, long-term employees. They generally work fewer hours than laborers in other countries—1,708 hours a year compared with 1,912 in the United States and 2,166 in Japan. They also enjoy greater benefits, such as medical care, vacation time, and maternity leave. By law, an employee is entitled to six weeks of paid sick leave each year. Pensions (retirement pay) are also high. German laws make working conditions fair, safe, and humane for most people.

The great majority of Germans are middle class. They are white-collar (office workers, executives) and blue-collar workers (laborers, tradespeople). Germany has a small group that is wealthy and a very small lower class.

Despite reunification, a steel worker in the western part of Germany, like the one pictured at right, will enjoy a shorter workweek and access to more high-tech equipment and facilities than fellow steel workers in the eastern half of the country.

Among the poorest residents of Germany are the 2 million foreign workers. Most foreigners work in heavy industry (such as steel and automobile production) and in the service industry (hotels and restaurants).

# Industries

Two-thirds of Germany's workers labor in the service industries. A service industry is any business or occupation that does not produce tangible goods (like radios, televisions, toys, or cars) but instead offers services that help people conduct their business and lives more easily and pleasurably. Members of the service industry include gas station owners, auto mechanics, hairdressers, teachers, salespeople, bus drivers, lawyers, dry cleaners, house and office cleaners, stockbrokers, and hundreds of other positions.

The second-largest sector of the German economy is manufacturing, or the making of goods that are bought and sold. This sector is especially important because goods that are manufactured can be sold to other countries, bringing foreign money into the country and enriching the economy. Germany's top manufacturing industries, in order, are machine tools, automobiles, electrical products, and chemicals. Other important products are iron, steel, coal, and airplanes.

Industrial production is spread throughout most of the nation. The large cities of Hanover, Munich, Frankfurt am Main, Leipzig, and Stuttgart have many factories. Southern Germany is home to most of the large automobile producers. Chemicals are made along the southern Rhine and the Elbe in the east. The largest industrial region of Europe is located along the Ruhr River in North Rhine-Westphalia.

Germany has several large, well-known manufacturers: Daimler-Benz, which makes

This is an espresso machine made by Krups, a German manufacturer of small home appliances. Other Krups products include coffeemakers, coffee grinders, toasters, kettles, juicers, waffle makers, blenders, and ice-cream makers.

Mercedes cars; Bavarian Motor Works (BMW); Volkswagen; Siemens, which makes electric products; and Bayer, the chemical company which makes aspirin, among many other products. Though North Americans are familiar with these industrial giants, 98 percent of Germany's manufacturers are small- and mid-sized businesses of 500 or fewer employees.

## Agriculture and Forestry

The third important sector of the German economy—agriculture and its related industries—is very tiny. It accounts for only about 2 percent of the country's wealth. In the flat northern lowlands, farmers grow wheat, barley, and sugar beets. The hilly uplands yield potatoes and vegetables. The southern mountains support the cattle and pigs that supply the nation's supply of milk, pork, and beef. And the river valleys of the south and west are carpeted with vineyards. In addition to the larger farms, small vegetable plots and fruit orchards surround the bigger cities.

A young girl milks a cow as part of an educational program on an organic farm in Germany. In 2002, there were 14,703 farmers operating organic farms across 1.56 million acres (632,165 hectares) of land. This represents 3.7 percent of the total available agricultural area and 3.2 percent of the total number of German farms. By 2010, the German government hopes to see 20 percent of Germany's agricultural land devoted to organic farming.

A shepherd in Bavaria carries a baby lamb on his shoulders. Seventy percent of Bavaria's agriculture is devoted to the raising of livestock such as cows, sheep, pigs, and horses.

Since almost a third of Germany is forested, the lumber industry is large. But it can meet only two-thirds of the country's lumber needs. Germany must import hardwoods. The vast stands of fir, pine, spruce, oak, and beech trees are among the country's greatest natural resources. Not only are German forests harvested for lumber, they are also used for the outdoor recreation Germans love. By law all forests, even those privately owned, are open to anyone for hiking and camping.

The health of German forests is very fragile, however. The manufacturing plants that helped rebuild the country in the postwar years of the 1950s and 1960s spewed toxic chemicals into the air. Those chemicals and the exhaust from cars mix with moisture and oxygen in the atmosphere to form acid rain. When this rain falls on forests and vegetation, it can damage or destroy them. By the time the problem was noticed in the 1970s, over half the trees of the forests were dead or sick. At that time, the government enacted strict laws to curb pollution. Today, the forests are beginning to recover.

## Reunification and the Future

Pollution has been an even greater problem since reunification. East Germany did not have the same strict environmental controls that West Germany did, and its air, rivers, and lakes were very unhealthy. Strip mining left great tracts of its land bare. Poor methods of waste disposal contaminated its soil and groundwater. In addition, the East German economy lagged far behind that of the West. East Germany's factories and equipment were old. Working conditions and standards of living were much better in the West. Since reunification, the western Länder have pumped millions of dollars into the Länder of the former East Germany, trying to bring the eastern half of the reunified country up to the same standards as the more modern and wealthy western half.

This former blast furnace in Duisburg is artistically lit in ever-shifting green, blue, and red colors. Once a thriving steel works and coal mining center, much of the complex has been shut down and converted into a large landscape park.

As exciting and emotional as reunification was, it caused friction between the two halves of Germany. Some East Germans resented being told that they were "behind" the West. They resented being the ones asked to do all the changing and catching up. Reunification made them free, but it also brought difficulties. Before, the East had full employment thanks to the economic controls of the Communist government. After reunification, unemployment rates soared, as antiquated and inefficient East German companies and factories were closed down. Instead of the security of government control over every aspect of society, the East began to experience increased homelessness, crime, and drug abuse. In some ways, easterners suddenly felt like foreigners in their own land, looked down upon by their wealthier neighbors and at the mercy of West German charity and jobs.

Despite the lingering tensions between the "two Germanys," however, reunification is progressing well. It may take decades to undo the effects of forty-five years of separation, but both halves are committed to being one. Despite their recent history of division, Germans from both east and west have a fierce pride in their shared cultural heritage. Easterners and westerners are both Germans, and Germans are disciplined, hard-working people. For centuries they maintained their traditions through tremendous social, political, and economic upheavals. Germans have a history of overcoming great problems, and doing so with enormous pride, creativity, and energy. These traits are Germany's greatest strength.

# GERMANY
## AT A GLANCE

## HISTORY

As the Huns swept from Asia across Europe in the fifth century, scattered Germanic tribes fled ahead of them, filling most of central and western Europe. Each tribe grew into its own tiny kingdom. In 800, Charlemagne, king of the Franks, had become the most powerful. Reasoning that all the German tribes were heir to the Roman Empire they had destroyed, Charlemagne had himself crowned emperor of the Romans. The empire survived through the course of several dynasties for a thousand years as the Holy Roman Empire. This later became known as the First Reich. In reality, however, the empire was never more than a loose association of independent German states.

Rivalry among the states, interference from the Catholic Church, the emergence of leagues of cities, and the Protestant Reformation kept the empire divided. The state of Prussia eventually emerged as the dominant German state. In 1871, the Prussian noble Otto von Bismarck was able to unite all the states under Wilhelm I, who became kaiser of the German Empire, the Second Reich. Germany remained a unified country for seventy-four years, until 1945.

In 1914, Germany plunged all of Europe into world war. The defeated country went from an empire to a republic—the Weimar Republic. The terms of the Versailles Treaty ending the conflict were harsh, and

Adolf Hitler leads a massive Nazi Party political rally in Germany.

the country was economically devastated. The demoralized Germans were ripe for a savior. In 1933, Adolf Hitler seemed to be that hero.

But Hitler's Nazi regime proved an even worse nightmare. In his twelve years in power, Hitler bankrupted the country morally and financially. To enlarge his realm he began World War II. He murdered millions of his own citizens, including about 6 million Jews, and was responsible for the deaths of millions more worldwide. His self-proclaimed Third Reich ended in shame and defeat in 1945.

After the war, Germany was divided into two countries: West Germany, a democracy, and East Germany, a Communist state under the control of the Soviet Union. Both countries wanted the city of Berlin, located in East Germany, so it was also divided. Because living conditions were more desirable in the west, many East Germans fled to West Germany. To keep from losing its workers, the Soviet-controlled Communists closed the borders of East Germany, refusing to allow people to leave. In the divided city of Berlin, a wall was erected for the same purpose.

The collapse of Communism in Eastern Europe in 1989 brought an end to the Berlin Wall. It brought the two halves of the divided country together again. On October 3, 1990, East and West Germany reunified, becoming the Federal Republic of Germany. The reunification process has not been easy, but it is proceeding well. Today, Germany is strong and peace-loving. It has an influential voice in international affairs and is a founding member of the European Union.

## ECONOMY

The German economy is heavily based on the service industries, such as hotels, restaurants, banks,

An employee of the Lichtwer Pharma AG drug company holds pills made from herbal and organic ingredients.

A fleet of new Mercedes Benz automobiles stands ready to roll out of the showroom.

investment houses, clothing stores, dry cleaners, hairdressers, and so forth. Heavy industry is Germany's second-largest source of revenue, while agriculture makes up only a small part of the economy. Almost 64 percent of Germany's 42 million workers are employed by the service industries, while 33.4 percent work in industries like iron and steel making, coal mining, electronics production, and car manufacturing. Only 3 percent of German workers are employed in agriculture-related activities, including farming.

Germany is among the world's largest and most technologically advanced producers of iron, steel, coal, cement, chemicals, machinery, cars and trucks, machine tools, and electronics. It is a world-famous producer of high-quality foods and beverages, including beer, wine, sausage, and pastries. Its shipbuilding and textiles industries are also thriving. Germany's gross domestic product (GDP; the total amount of goods and services produced in a year) is over $2 trillion. The service industries account for 68 percent of Germany's GDP, while heavy industry contributes to 31 percent of the total. Agriculture represents only 1 percent of the goods and services produced in Germany every year.

## GOVERNMENT AND POLITICS

Germany is officially known as the Federal Republic of Germany (Bundesrepublik Deutschland). A federal republic is a government in which a nation's citizens elect officers or representatives to govern them, make laws, and look after their interests. A republic is led not by a king or queen, but by a chief of state (usually a prime minister or president who is also elected). Germany's chief of state is the president. Its head of government is the chancellor. The president, who is less powerful than the chancellor, is elected to a five-year term by a Federal Convention that includes the members of the Federal

Assembly and an equal number of delegates elected by state parliaments. The chancellor is elected to a four-year term by the Federal Assembly.

Germany's legislative branch is a two-house parliament. One house, the Federal Assembly (Bundestag), has 603 seats. Assembly members are elected by popular vote (the voting age is eighteen). The sixty-nine representatives of the other house, the Federal Council (Bundesrat), are elected by the governments of the sixteen German states (Länder). Germany's judicial branch is called the Federal Constitutional

In 1999, the renovated and rebuilt Reichstag once again became the seat of Germany's Bundestag, a role it had not filled since World War II.

Court (Bundesverfassungsgericht). Half of its judges are elected by the Bundestag, and the other half are chosen by the Bundesrat. Germany's new constitution, based on the Basic Law adopted by West Germany in 1949, was signed on October 3, 1990, the official date of German reunification.

# TIMELINE

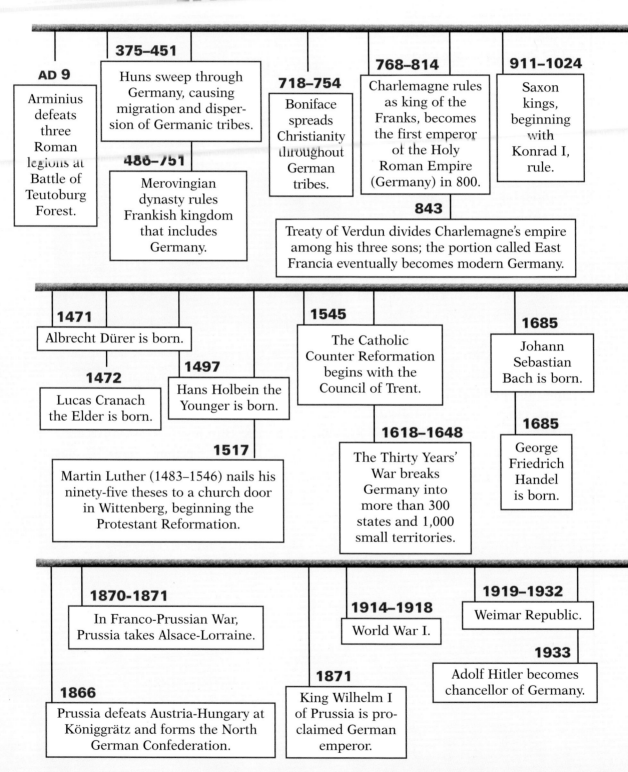

**AD 9**
Arminius defeats three Roman legions at Battle of Teutoburg Forest.

**375–451**
Huns sweep through Germany, causing migration and dispersion of Germanic tribes.

**486–751**
Merovingian dynasty rules Frankish kingdom that includes Germany.

**718–754**
Boniface spreads Christianity throughout German tribes.

**768–814**
Charlemagne rules as king of the Franks, becomes the first emperor of the Holy Roman Empire (Germany) in 800.

**911–1024**
Saxon kings, beginning with Konrad I, rule.

**843**
Treaty of Verdun divides Charlemagne's empire among his three sons; the portion called East Francia eventually becomes modern Germany.

**1471**
Albrecht Dürer is born.

**1472**
Lucas Cranach the Elder is born.

**1497**
Hans Holbein the Younger is born.

**1517**
Martin Luther (1483–1546) nails his ninety-five theses to a church door in Wittenberg, beginning the Protestant Reformation.

**1545**
The Catholic Counter Reformation begins with the Council of Trent.

**1618–1648**
The Thirty Years' War breaks Germany into more than 300 states and 1,000 small territories.

**1685**
Johann Sebastian Bach is born.

**1685**
George Friedrich Handel is born.

**1870-1871**
In Franco-Prussian War, Prussia takes Alsace-Lorraine.

**1866**
Prussia defeats Austria-Hungary at Königgrätz and forms the North German Confederation.

**1871**
King Wilhelm I of Prussia is proclaimed German emperor.

**1914–1918**
World War I.

**1919–1932**
Weimar Republic.

**1933**
Adolf Hitler becomes chancellor of Germany.

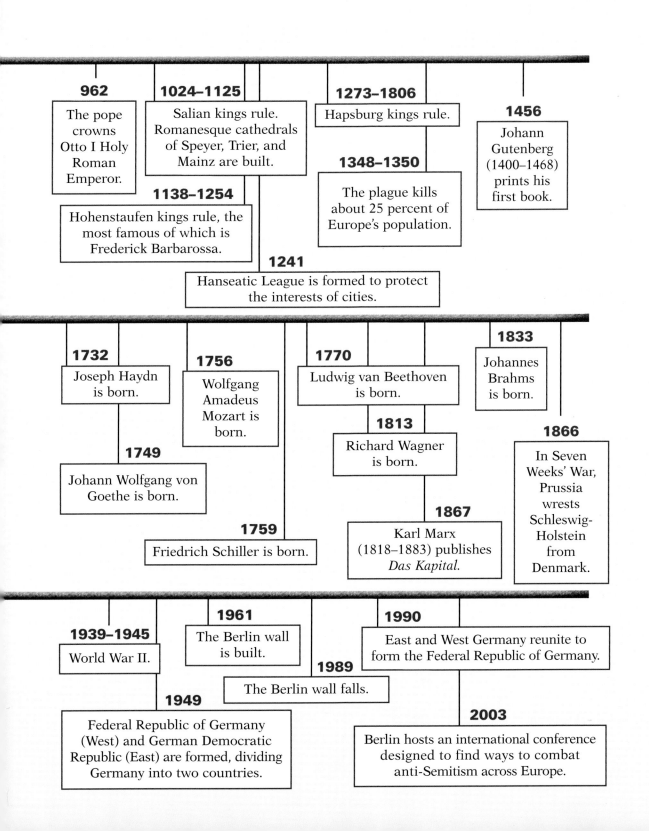

**962**
The pope crowns Otto I Holy Roman Emperor.

**1024–1125**
Salian kings rule. Romanesque cathedrals of Speyer, Trier, and Mainz are built.

**1138–1254**
Hohenstaufen kings rule, the most famous of which is Frederick Barbarossa.

**1241**
Hanseatic League is formed to protect the interests of cities.

**1273–1806**
Hapsburg kings rule.

**1348–1350**
The plague kills about 25 percent of Europe's population.

**1456**
Johann Gutenberg (1400–1468) prints his first book.

**1732**
Joseph Haydn is born.

**1749**
Johann Wolfgang von Goethe is born.

**1756**
Wolfgang Amadeus Mozart is born.

**1759**
Friedrich Schiller is born.

**1770**
Ludwig van Beethoven is born.

**1813**
Richard Wagner is born.

**1867**
Karl Marx (1818–1883) publishes *Das Kapital*.

**1833**
Johannes Brahms is born.

**1866**
In Seven Weeks' War, Prussia wrests Schleswig-Holstein from Denmark.

**1939–1945**
World War II.

**1949**
Federal Republic of Germany (West) and German Democratic Republic (East) are formed, dividing Germany into two countries.

**1961**
The Berlin wall is built.

**1989**
The Berlin wall falls.

**1990**
East and West Germany reunite to form the Federal Republic of Germany.

**2003**
Berlin hosts an international conference designed to find ways to combat anti-Semitism across Europe.

# GERMANY

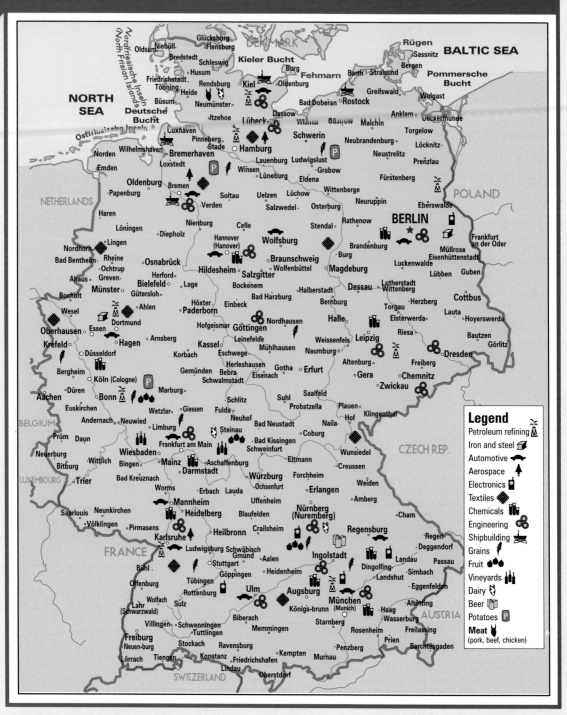

**Legend**

- Petroleum refining
- Iron and steel
- Automotive
- Aerospace
- Electronics
- Textiles
- Chemicals
- Engineering
- Shipbuilding
- Grains
- Fruit
- Vineyards
- Dairy
- Beer
- Potatoes
- **Meat** (pork, beef, chicken)

# ECONOMIC FACT SHEET

**GDP in US$:** $2.184 trillion

**GDP Sectors:** Agriculture 1%, industry 31%, services 68%

**Land Use:** Arable land 33.88%, permanent crops 0.65%, forests 29.2%, other 36.27%

**Currency:** Euro (the common currency of the European Union, replaced the Deutsche Mark on January 1, 2002): .807 euros to the U.S. dollar (2004)

**Workforce:** Agriculture 2.8%, industry 33.4%, services 63.8%

**Major Agricultural Products:** Potatoes, wheat, barley, sugar beets, fruit, cabbages, cattle, pigs, poultry

**Major Exports:** $608 billion—machinery, vehicles, chemicals, metals and manufactures, foodstuffs, textiles

**Major Imports:** $487.3 billion—machinery, vehicles, chemicals, foodstuffs, textiles, metals

*Significant Trading Partners*:

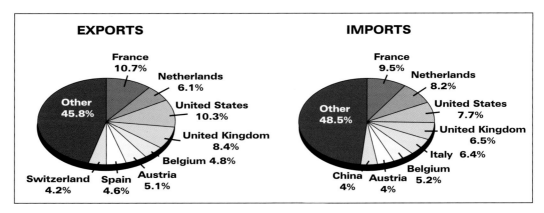

**Rate of Unemployment:** 9.8 % (2002)

**Highways:** Total 407,706 miles (656,140 km)

**Railroads:** Total 28,281 miles (45,514 km)

**Waterways**: Total 4,660 miles (7,500 km)

**Airports:** 551 (328 paved, 223 unpaved), heliports 40

# POLITICAL FACT SHEET

**Official Country Name:** The Federal Republic of Germany (Bundesrepublik Deutschland)

**Capital:** Berlin

**System of Government:** Federal Republic

**Federal Structure:** Chancellor, president, cabinet (ministers recommended by chancellor and appointed by president), a parliament made

up of the Federal Assembly and the Federal Council.

**Government Structure:** The Federal Assembly has 603 seats, and its representatives are elected by popular vote. The Federal Council has 69 seats, and its members are elected by Germany's state governments.

**National Anthem:** The third stanza of the poem *Das Lied der Deutschen*, written in 1841 by August Heinrich Hoffmann von Fallersleben and set to the melody of a song by Franz Joseph Haydn. The song was officially proclaimed the Federal Republic of Germany's national anthem in 1952.

> *Unity and right and freedom for the German Fatherland,*
> *For this let us all fraternally strive, each with heart and hand.*
> *Unity and right and freedom are the pledge of happiness.*
> *Bloom in the splendor of this happiness, Germany, our Fatherland.*

**Administrative Divisions:** (Sixteen states, or Länder): Baden-Württemberg, Bavaria, Berlin, Brandenburg, Bremen, Hamburg, Hessen, Lower Saxony, Mecklenburg-Vorpommern, North Rhine-Westphalia, Rhineland-Palatinate, Saarland, Saxony, Saxony-Anhalt, Schleswig-Holstein, and Thuringia.

**Independence:** October 3, 1990 (the day of German reunification, known as Unity Day)

**Constitution:** West Germany's Basic Law of May 23, 1949, was signed as reunified Germany's constitution on October 3, 1990.

**Legal System:** Civil law system with indigenous concepts; judicial review of legislative acts

**Suffrage:** Eighteen years of age; universal

**Number of Registered Voters:** 60,710,333 out of a population of 82,398,326 as of 2002

# CULTURAL FACT SHEET

**Official Languages:** German

**Major Religions:** Protestant 34%, Catholic 34%, Muslim 3.7%, Jewish 0.18%, unaffiliated or other 28.3%

**Population:** 82,398,326 (2003)

**Ethnic Groups:** German 91.5% (including minority groups: 120,000 Sorbs, 60,000 Danes, 12,000 Frisians, 70,000 Sinti and Roma), Turkish 2.4%, other (mostly Serbo-Croatian, Italian, Russian, Greek, Polish, and Spanish) 6.1%

**Life Expectancy:** Total 78.42 years

**Time**: Germany is Greenwich Mean Time + one hour

**Literacy Rate:** 99%

**Cultural Leaders:**

**Visual Arts:** Joseph Beuys, Lucian Freud, Andreas Gursky, Helmut Newton, Sigmar Polke, Gerhard Richter, Kiki Smith, Thomas Struth, Mies van der Rohe

**Literature:** Jürgen Becker, Maxim Biller, Thomas Brussig, Hans Magnus Enzensberger, Günter Grass, Gerhard Kopf, Michael Kruger, Thomas Mann, Lilli Palmer, Ingo Schulze

**Entertainment:** Moritz Bleibtreu, Bruno Ganz, Oliver Hirschbiegel, Juliane Köhler, Ute Lemper, Caroline Link, Wolfgang Petersen, Franka Potente, Tom Tykwer, Wim Wenders

**Sports:** Anni Friesinger (speed skating), Oliver Kahn (soccer), Gunda Niemann-Stirnemann (speed skating), Michael Schumacher (Formula One racing), Hannah Stockbauer (swimming), Erik Zabel (cycling)

## National Holidays and Festivals

**January 1: Neujahr (New Year's Day)**

**February-March: Fasching or Karneval** (a pre-Lent celebration)

**April 30: Walpurgisnacht (Walpurgis Night)** (a Halloween-like holiday designed to scare away witches, devils, and other evil spirits)

**May 1: Tag der Arbeit/Erster Mai** (Labor Day)

**Late September–early October: Oktoberfest**

**October 3: Tag der deutschen Einheit (Day of German Unity)** (commemorates the reunification of East and West Germany)

**November 11: Martinstag (Martinmas, Saint Martin's Day)** (commemoration of a popular European saint combined with elements of Halloween and Thanksgiving. The unofficial kickoff to the official start of Fasching).

**December 6: Nikolaustag (Saint Nicholas Day)** (a day on which children receive gifts from the Santa Claus-like European Saint)

**December 24: Heiligabend (Christmas Eve)**

**December 25: Weihnachten (Christmas Day)**

**December 26: Zweiter Weihnachtstag or Stephanstag (The Second Day of Christmas or Saint Stephen's Day)**

**December 31: Silvester (New Year's Eve)**

# GLOSSARY

**altarpiece (AHL-tur-pees)** A painting on or behind the altar in a church.

**asylum (uh-SY-lum)** Protection from arrest in one country granted to a person taking refuge in another country.

**epic (EH-pik)** A story, usually long and in verse, about the deeds of heroes or gods.

**façade (fuh-SAHD)** The front, main, or most conspicuous part of a building.

**fjord (FEE-ord)** A long, narrow inlet of the sea with high, rocky banks.

**fresco (FRES-ko)** A painting made on a plaster wall.

**gorge (GORJ)** A narrow passage between hills or mountains.

**guild (GILD)** An association of people, usually tradesmen or craftsmen, engaged in the same activities.

**Gulf Stream (GULF STREEM)** The warm ocean current that flows from the Gulf of Mexico up the U.S. coast, then across the Atlantic Ocean to northern Europe.

**heath (HEETH)** A large area of open land overgrown with shrubs.

**heresy (HAYR-uh-see)** Religious beliefs that are different from the conventional or official beliefs taught by an established church.

**imperial (im-PEER-ee-ul)** Having to do with an empire or emperor.

**margrave (MAR-grayv)** A nobleman, an official of the king.

**moor (MOR)** A tract of land that is often marshy and sometimes covered with shrubs.

**oompah (OOM-pa)** A kind of music produced by traditional Bavarian brass bands.

**orthodox (OR-thuh-doks)** Conforming to commonly accepted and established doctrines.

**per capita (PER KAP-uh-tuh)** Per person (literally, per head).

**plateau (plah-TOW)** A stretch of level land that is elevated but flat.

**Reich (RIKE)** The German word for realm or kingdom.

**repatriate (ree-PAY-tree-ayt)** A person who has returned to his or her country.

**terrace (TEHR-us)** A hilly or mountainous land that has level steps.

**tributary (TRI-bu-ter-ee)** A smaller river flowing into a larger river.

# FOR MORE INFORMATION

German Culture Center
University of Missouri-St. Louis
#50 TCC Building
8001 Natural Bridge Road
St. Louis, MO 63121-4499
(314) 516-6620
Web site: http://germanculturecenter.org

German National Tourist Office
Chanin Building, 52nd Floor
122 East 42nd Street
New York, NY 10168-0072
(212) 661-7200
(800) 651-7010
Web site: http://www.cometogermany.com

German Studies Association
340 E 15th Street
Tempe, AZ 85281 USA
(480) 966-2245
Web site: http://www.g-s-a.org

## Web Sites

Due to the changing nature of Internet links, the Rosen Publishing Group, Inc., has developed an online list of Web sites related to the subject of this book. This site is updated regularly. Please use this link to access the list:

http://www.rosenlinks.com/pswc/germ

# FOR FURTHER READING

Arnold, Helen. *Germany*. New York: Raintree/Steck-Vaughn, 1996.

Blashfield, Jean F. *Germany*. New York: Children's Press, 2003.

Catucci, Stefano. *Bach and Baroque Music*. Hauppauge, NY: Barrons Educational Series, 1998.

Clark, Cherese, and Charles Clark. *Life in Berlin*. Farmington Hills, MI: Gale Group, 2001.

Dudman, John. *Division of Berlin*. Vero Beach, FL: Rourke, 1998.

Frost, Helen. *A Look at Germany*. Mankato, MN: Pebble Books, 2002.

Hieman, Sarah. *Germany ABCs: A Book About the People and Places of Germany*. Minneapolis, MN: Picture Window Books, 2003.

Kitchen, Martin. *The Cambridge Illustrated History of Germany*. New York: Cambridge University Press, 1997.

Lane, Kathryn. *Germany: The Culture*. New York: Crabtree Publishing, 2001.

Lane, Kathryn. *Germany: The Land*. New York: Crabtree Publishing, 2001.

Lane, Kathryn. *Germany: The People*. New York: Crabtree Publishing, 2001.

Lee, Stephen J. *Imperial Germany 1871–1918*. New York: Routledge, 1998.

McGowen, Tom. *Frederick the Great, Bismarck, and the Building of the German Empire in World History*. Berkeley Heights, NJ: Enslow, 2002.

Rogasky, Barbara. *Smoke and Ashes: The Story of the Holocaust*. New York: Holiday House, 2002.

Spencer, William. *Germany Then and Now*. Danbury, CT: Franklin Watts, 1994.

Zuehlke, Jeffrey. *Germany in Pictures*. Minneapolis, MN: Lerner Publications Co., 2003.

# BIBLIOGRAPHY

Ardagh, John. *Germany and the Germans: The United Germany in the Mid-1990s*. New York: Penguin Books, 1996.

Craig, Gordon A. *The Germans*. New York: Penguin Books, 1991.

Cross, Robert. "The Oberammergau Passion Play Has a New Script," *Detroit Free Press*, July 2, 2000.

Fallon, Steve, and Anthony Haywood, Andrea Schulte-Peevers, Nick Selby. *Germany*. Oakland, CA: Lonely Planet, 1998.

Faßke, Helmut. *Die Sorben in Deutschland* (trans. Heather Watson). Bautzen, Saxony, Federal Republic of Germany: Macica Serbska, 1991.

Flippo, Hyde. *The German Way: Aspects of Behavior, Attitudes, and Customs in the German-Speaking World*. New York: McGraw-Hill, 1996.

Fulbrook, Mary. *A Concise History of Germany*. New York: Cambridge University Press, 1991.

Hagood, Susan. "Germany: Where Roads and Wildlife Coexist." Federal Highway Administration. Summer 2002. Retrieved November 2003 (http:// www.fhwa.dot.gov/ environmentgreenerroadsides/ sum02p3.htm).

Hooven, Stacey van. "The ABCs of the German School System." *Expaticia*. 2003. Retrieved November 2003 (http://www.expatica.com/ germanymain.asp?HRSite=&pad= 202,222,&item_id=9598).

Midgette, Anne. "Estival Festivals: Summer Musical Pleasures in German-Speaking Europe." German Life Online. June-July 1996. Retrieved November 2003 (http://www.germanlife. com/ Archives/1996/9606_01. html).

"Religion." German Embassy, Washington D.C. 2001–2003. Retrieved November 2003 (http:// www.germany-info.org/relaunch/ culture/life/religion.html).

Schulze, Hagen. *Germany: A New History*. Cambridge, MA: Harvard University Press, 2001.

Shirer, William L. *The Rise and Fall of the Third Reich*. New York: Simon and Schuster, 1990.

Thornhill, Robert. "Turkish Delight: Forget Bratwurst and Big Macs— Döner Kebab Is Germany's Fast Food." German Life Online. August/ September 1999. Retrieved November 2003 (http://www.germanlife.com/ Archives/1999/9908_01.htm).

U.S. Central Intelligence Agency. *The World Factbook: Germany*. August 2003. Retrieved November 2003 (http://www.odci.gov/cia/publications/ factbook/geos/gm.html).

# PRIMARY SOURCE IMAGE LIST

**Page 6:** Neuschwanstein Castle in Bavaria, built by King Ludwig II between 1869 and 1886.

**Page 10:** Saint Coloman Church, near Fussen, Bavaria, built between 1350 and 1400 and enlarged in 1685.

**Page 19:** Sixth-century BC Germanic silver and garnet jewelry. Housed in the Victoria and Albert Museum, London, England.

**Page 21 (bottom):** Color engraved manuscript page from the 1543 manuscript *The Origin of the First Twelve Old Kings and Princes of the German Nation*. Housed in the Ammon Stapleton Collection at Penn State University.

**Page 23:** Detail of Charlemagne and his wife from a circa 800 manuscript. Housed in the Abbey Library of Sankt Paul im Lavanttal in Austria.

**Page 24 (top):** Charlemagne's signature on a woodcut from 790.

**Page 24 (bottom):** Remains of a second-century Roman amphitheater, Trier, Germany.

**Page 25:** Woodcut print by Michael Wohlgemuth of medieval Cologne from the circa 1493 manuscript *Liber Chronicarum*.

**Page 26:** The Final Act of the Congress of Vienna, signed on June 9, 1815. Housed in the Archives du Ministere des Affaires Etrangeres, Paris.

**Page 27:** *The Congress of Vienna*, 1814 engraving by Jean Baptiste Isabey. Housed in the Museo del Risorgimento in Milan, Italy.

**Page 28:** Circa 1890 photograph of Otto von Bismarck and his dogs. Housed in the IBA Collection.

**Page 29:** 1916 photograph of German soldiers stationed in a trench during World War I from the estate of Maurice Levert. Housed in the Coll. Archiv f. Kunst & Geschichte, Berlin.

**Page 30 (top):** *One People, One Country, One Leader!* Circa 1940 lithograph.

**Page 30 (bottom):** 1945 photograph of slave laborers in the Buchenwald concentration camp near Jena, Germany. Housed in the National Archives in Washington, D.C.

**Page 31:** 1945 photograph by Yevgeny Khaldei of a Soviet soldier raising the flag of the Soviet Union over the Reichstag in Berlin, Germany.

**Page 32 (top):** 1961 photograph by Burt Glinn of East German soldiers beginning construction of the Berlin wall.

**Page 32 (bottom):** 1989 photograph by Raymond Depardon of a West German man peering over the Berlin wall into East Berlin soon before the wall was torn down.

**Page 33:** 1989 photograph by Rene Burri of East and West German protesters gathered near the Brandenburg Gate and climbing on top of the Berlin wall.

**Page 40:** Fourteenth-century letter bearing the seal of Louis IV, German king and Holy Roman Emperor. Housed in the library of the University of Heidelberg.

**Page 41 (top):** Handwritten German translation of the Bible by Martin Luther, circa 1530. Housed in the Forschungsbibliothek in Gotha, Germany.

**Page 41 (bottom):** Mid-nineteenth-century engraving of Jacob Ludwig Carl Grimm and Wilhelm Carl Grimm.

**Page 44:** Illustrated cover of 1885 edition of *Kinder und Hausmärchen* (Children's and Household Tales), published in Berlin.

**Page 46:** Illuminated page from a fifteenth-century manuscript of the *Nibelungenlied*. Housed in the Staatsbibliothek, Berlin.

**Page 47:** Circa 1180 miniature of Frederick I (Barbarossa), German king and Holy Roman Emperor. Housed in the Landesbibliothek, Fulda, Germany.

**Page 48 (bottom):** Circa sixth-century reliquary of Theodoric the Great, king of the Ostrogoths. Housed in the Treasury of Monza Cathedral, Italy.

**Page 52:** 1884 program cover for the eighth annual Bayreuth Festival held in Bayreuth, Germany.

**Page 60:** Manuscript illustration depicting Saint Boniface's christening of the Teutons and his martyrdom at the hands of the Frisians. Housed in the library of the University of Göttingen.

**Page 61 (top):** 1539 portrait of Martin Luther by Lucas Cranach the Elder.

**Page 61 (bottom):** Sixteenth-century woodcut depicting Martin Luther writing his ninety-five theses on the door of Castle Church in Wittenberg, Germany.

**Page 62:** Wartburg Castle, built in 1067 by Duke Ludwig of Thuringia and renovated in the nineteenth century, overlooks the city of Eisenach in Thuringia, Germany.

**Page 67:** 1818 oil painting *Wanderer Above the Sea and Fog* by Caspar David Friedrich. Housed in the Kuntshalle in Hamburg, Germany.

**Page 68:** Illuminated manuscript page, depicting Holy Roman Emperor Otto III enthroned, from the circa 998 Gospels of Otto. Housed in the Bayerische Staatsbibliothek in Munich, Germany.

**Page 69:** Saint Michael's Church, built between 1010 and 1020 in Hildesheim, Germany.

**Page 71 (top):** 1498 self-portrait painted on wood by Albrecht Dürer. Housed in the Museo del Prado, Madrid, Spain.

**Page 71 (bottom):** Albrecht Dürer's *Lamentation Over the Dead Christ*, circa 1500 to 1503. Housed in the Alte Pinakothek in Munich, Germany.

**Page 72:** Circa 1747 center fresco of the Wies Church (Wieskirche) in Wies, Bavaria, Germany.

**Page 74:** Neue Nationalgalerie in Berlin, Germany, designed and built by Mies van der Rohe in 1968.

**Page 75:** *Bryce Canyon Translation*, painting by Max Ernst, 1946. Housed in the Sao Paulo Art Museum in Sao Paulo, Brazil.

**Page 76:** 1764 portrait of Johann Sebastian Bach by Elias Gottlieb Haussmann. Housed in the Museum der Bildenden Kuenste in Leipzig, Germany.

**Page 77:** Music print for the piano edition of the *Liebeslieder Walzer* by Johannes Brahms, published by N. Simrock GmbH, in Berlin and Leipzig, Germany.

**Page 78:** Page from handwritten manuscript of the *Hildebrandslied*, circa 850. Housed in the Hessische Landesbibliothek Kassel in Wiesbaden, Germany.

**Page 79 (bottom):** Thirteenth-century illustration from *Der Grosser Heidelberger Handschrift* depicting a German singing contest presided over by Landgraf Hermann von Thuringen, including minnesingers Wolfram von Eschenbach and Walther von der Vogelweide.

**Page 80:** Title page of a 1546 German version of the New Testament translated by Martin Luther and printed by Hans Lufft.

**Page 81 (top):** Manuscript page of a Johann Sebastian Bach prelude he gave to his wife as a gift. Housed in the Landesbibliothek in Wiesbaden, Germany.

**Page 81 (bottom):** 1756 oil-on-canvas portrait of Georg Friedrich Handel by Thomas Hudson. Housed in the National Portrait Gallery, London, England.

**Page 82 (top):** Nineteenth-century print of Faust and Mephistopheles from Goethe's *Faust*.